GRAND CANYON

a photographic journey

photography by Larry Lindahl

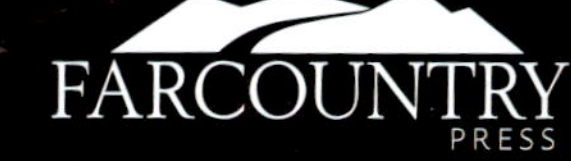

Right: Globemallow blooms along the Tanner Trail.

Far right: The morning sun bursts upon the South Rim at Hopi Point.

Title page: Sunrise gilds Mary Colter's Lookout Studio on the South Rim.

Front cover: A double rainbow scythes into the canyon over Vishnu Temple from Shoshone Point.

Back cover: At Navajo Point, the eye can wander from lichen to sunrise on distant buttes.

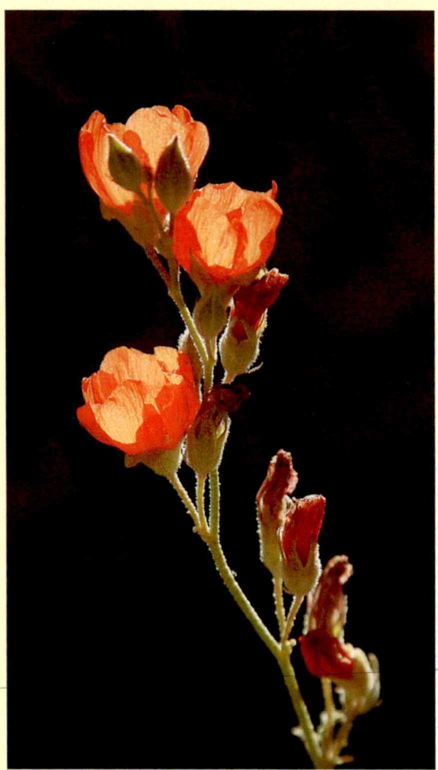

ISBN: 978-1-56037-843-3

Design by Steph Lehmann

For more information about our books, write Farcountry Press, P.O. Box 5630, Helena, MT 59604; call (800) 821-3874;
or visit www.farcountrypress.com.

Produced in the United States of America.
Printed in China.

28 27 26 25 24 1 2 3 4 5

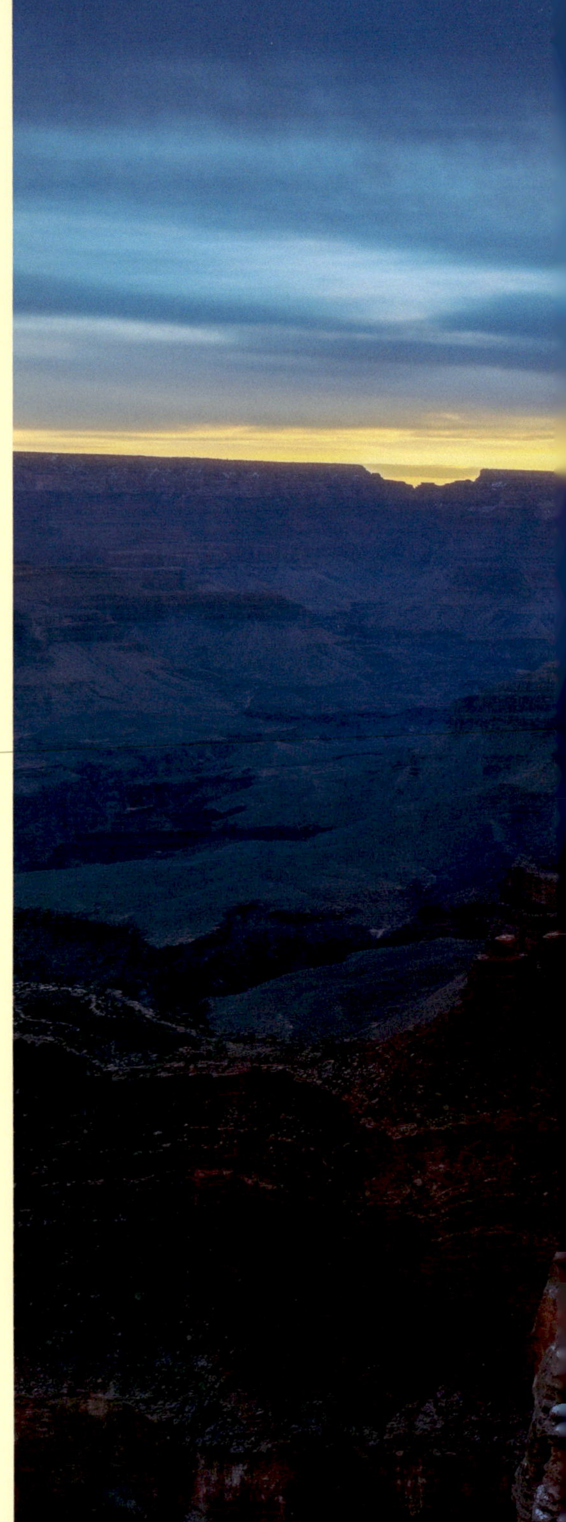

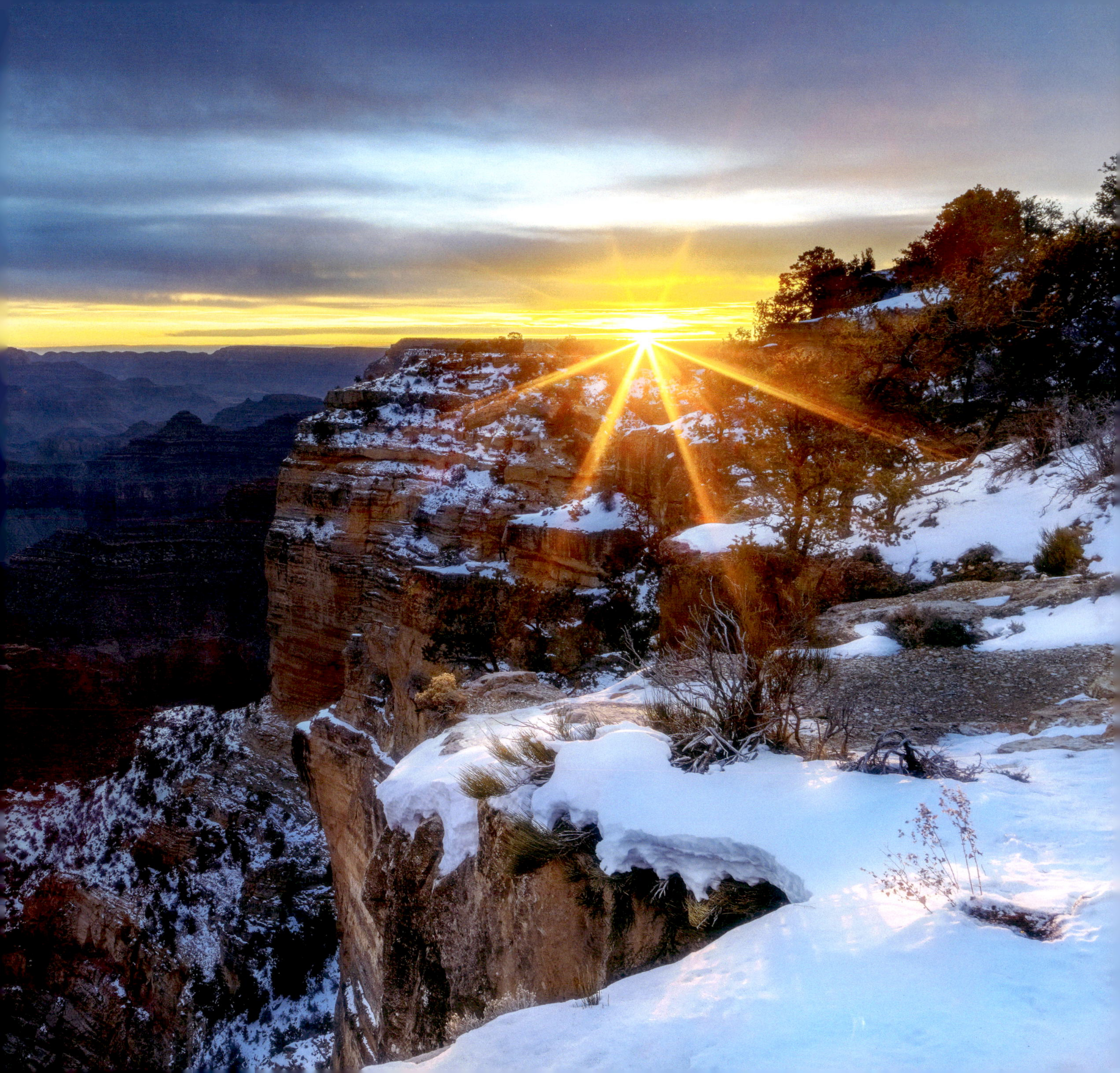

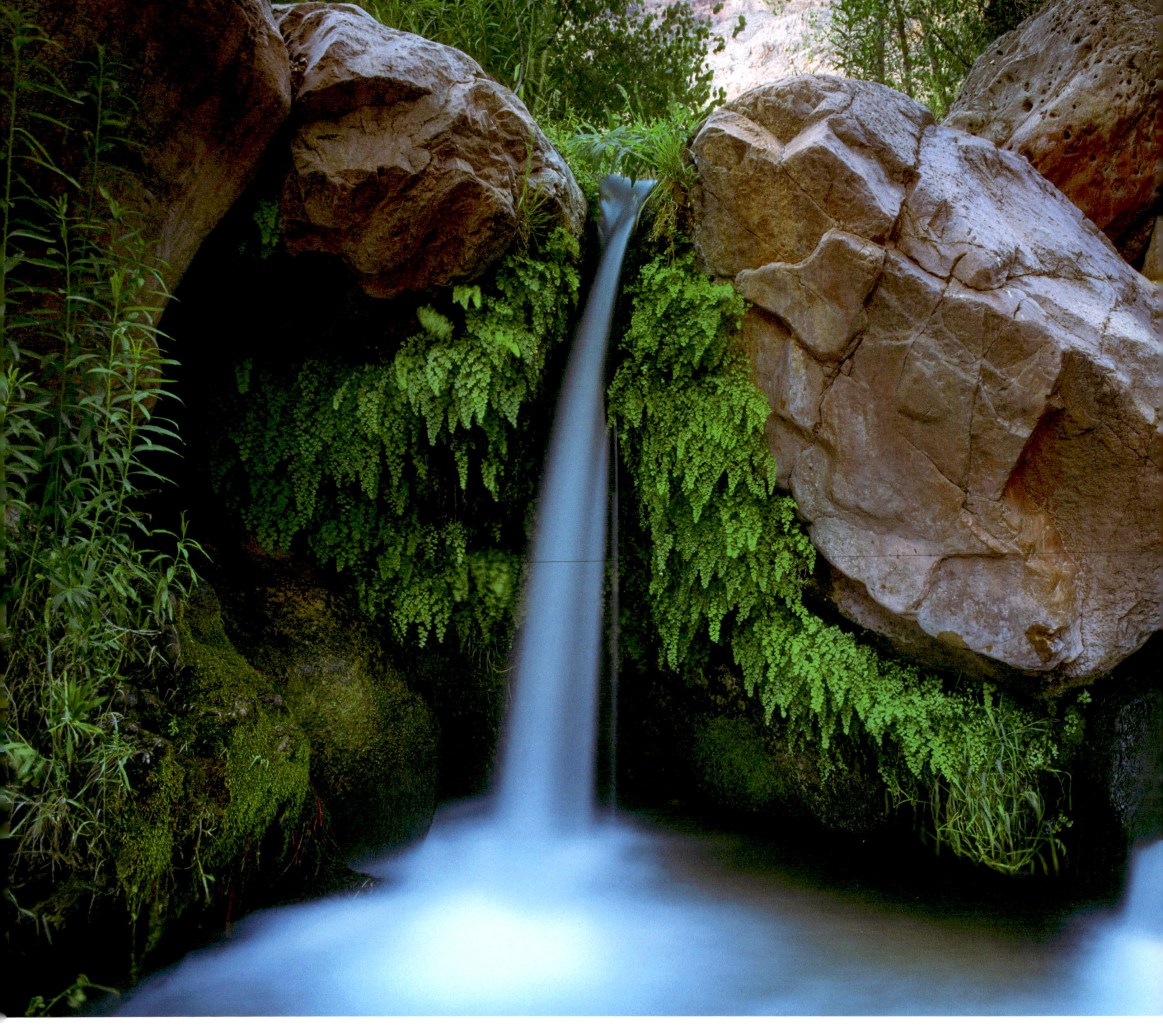

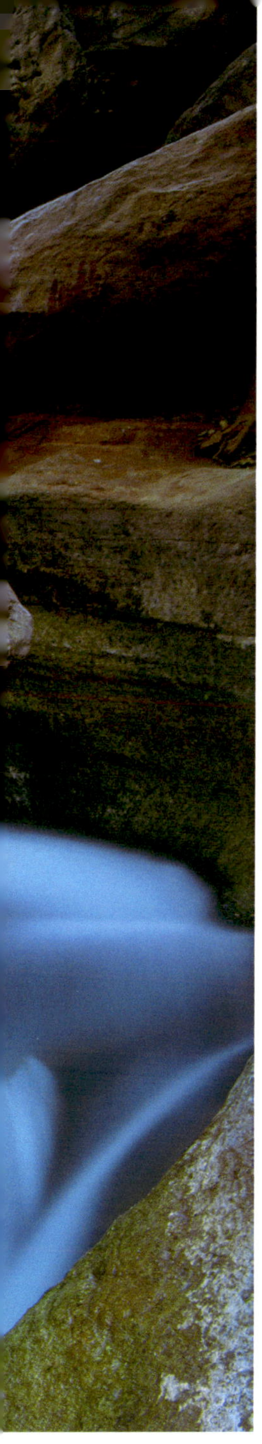

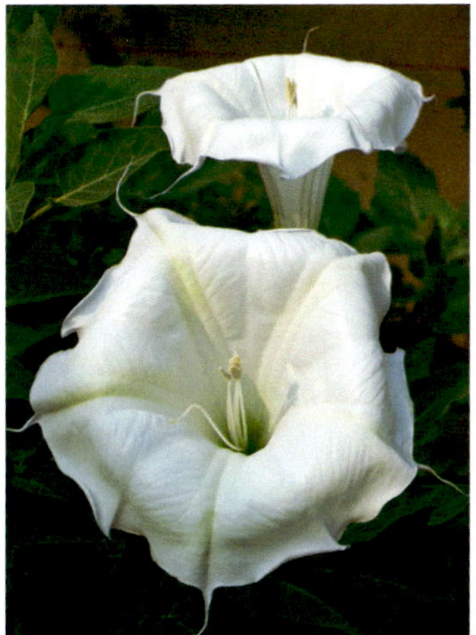

Left: Beautiful but deadly, sacred datura is a member of the nightshade family. From April to October, it blooms from evening to morning along roadsides and sandy arroyos.

Far left: Maidenhair ferns bedeck a small waterfall on upper Deer Creek beneath the Kaibab Plateau.

Below: Spray from Phantom Creek, a tributary of Bright Angel Creek, creates a cool microclimate.

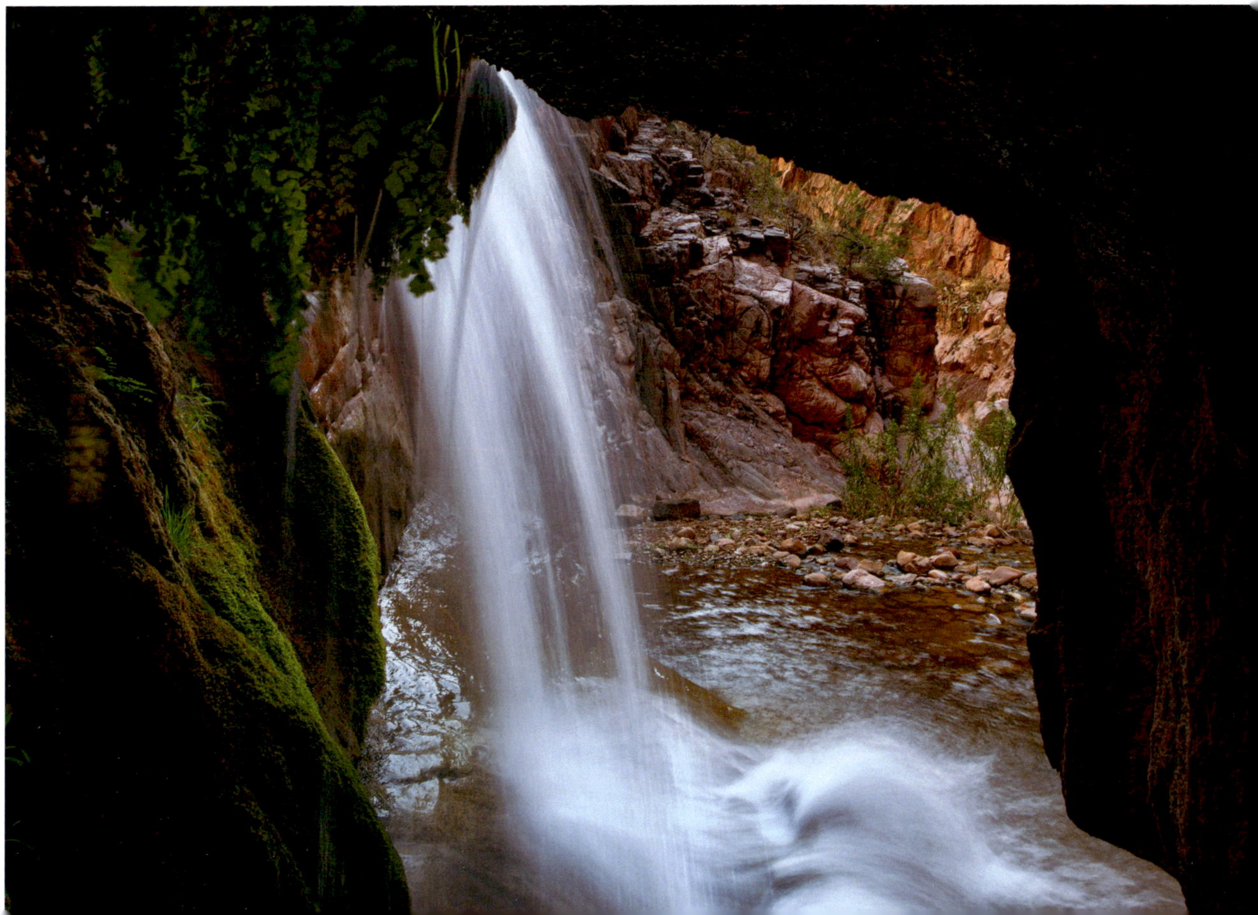

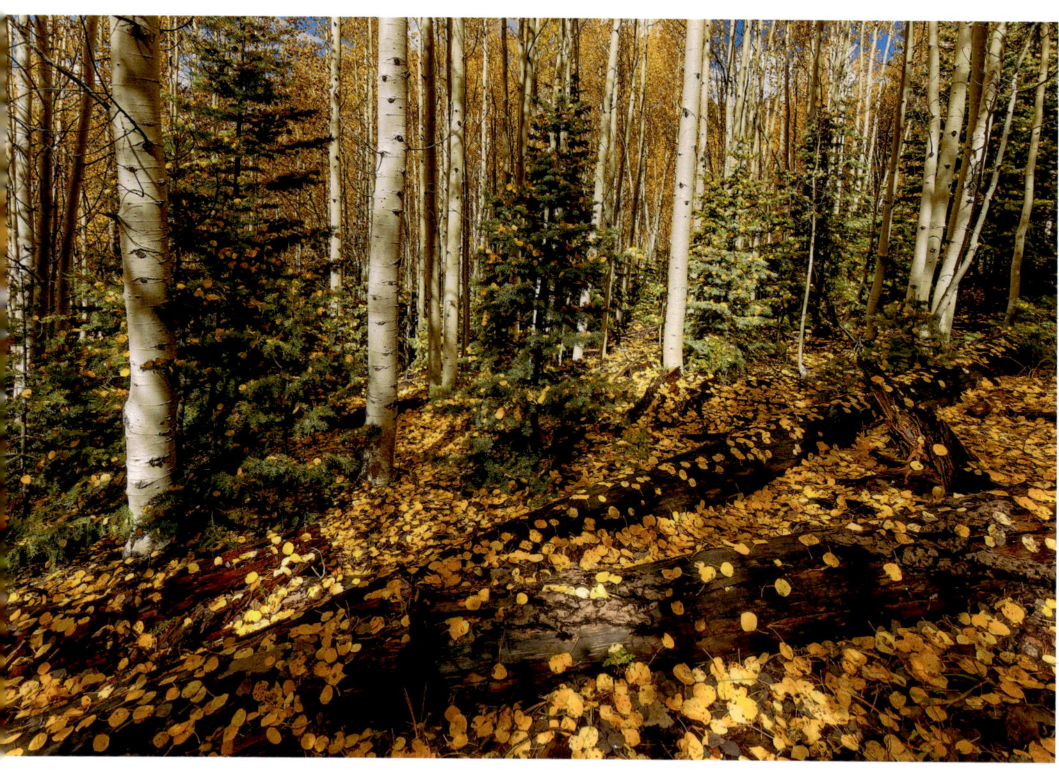

Above and far right: Aspen thrive in moist habitat on the North Rim.

Right: Near the confluence with Phantom Creek, the clear waters of Bright Angel Creek polish cobbles in the streambed.

Following pages: Daybreak warms Wotans Throne at Cape Royal on the North Rim.

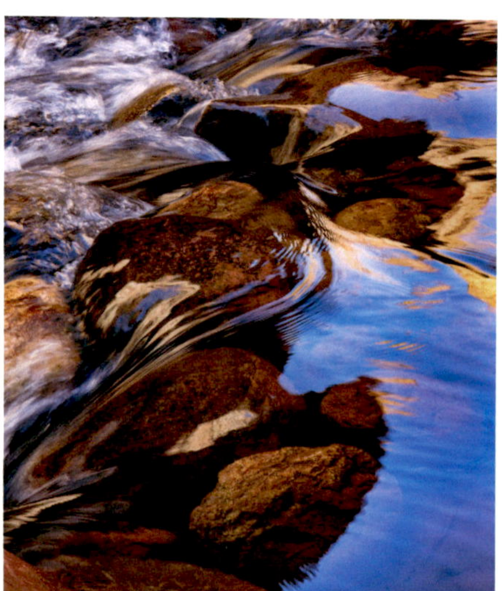

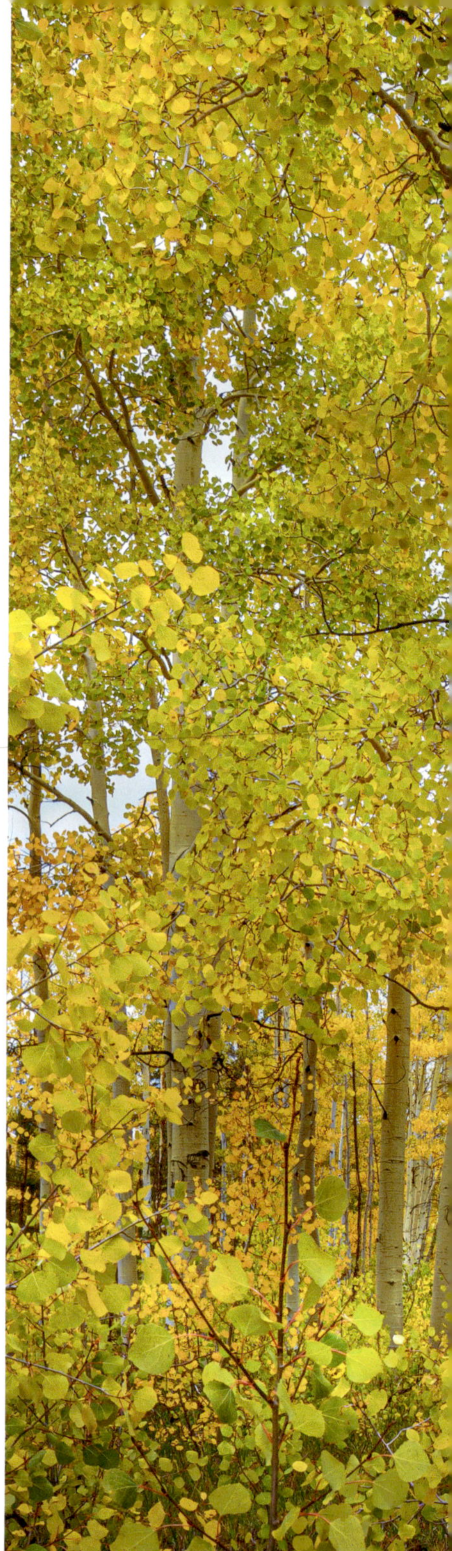

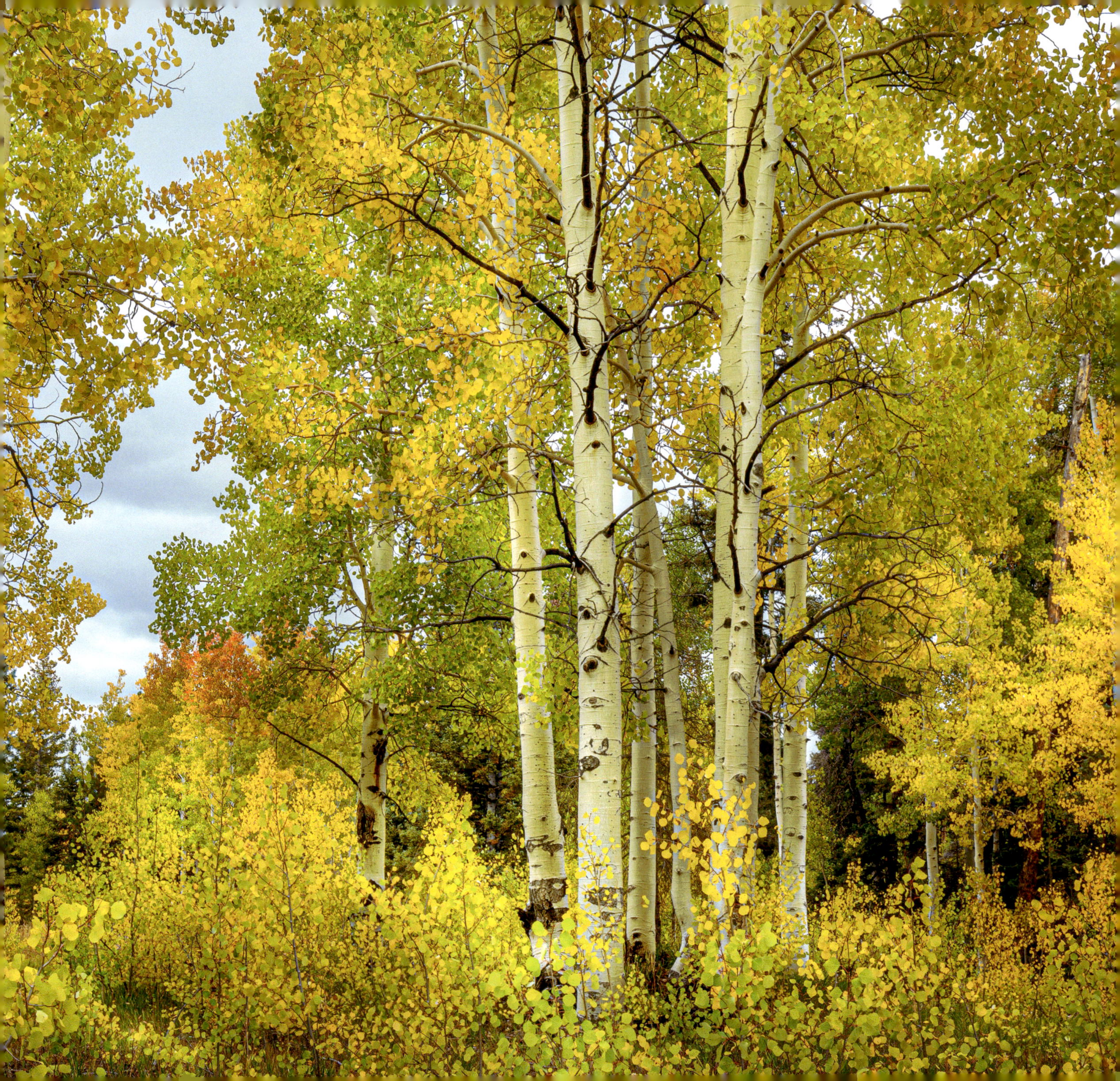

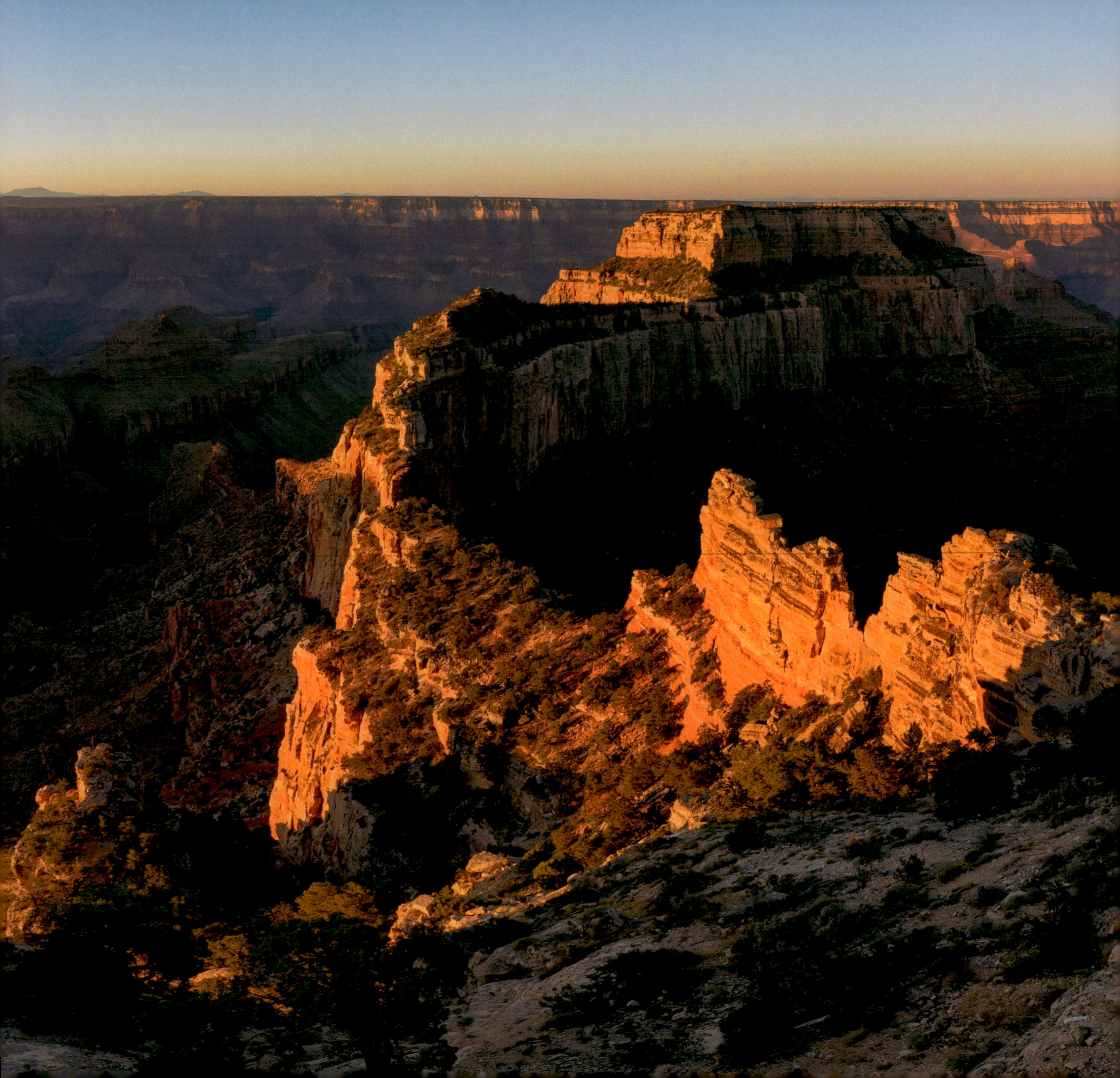

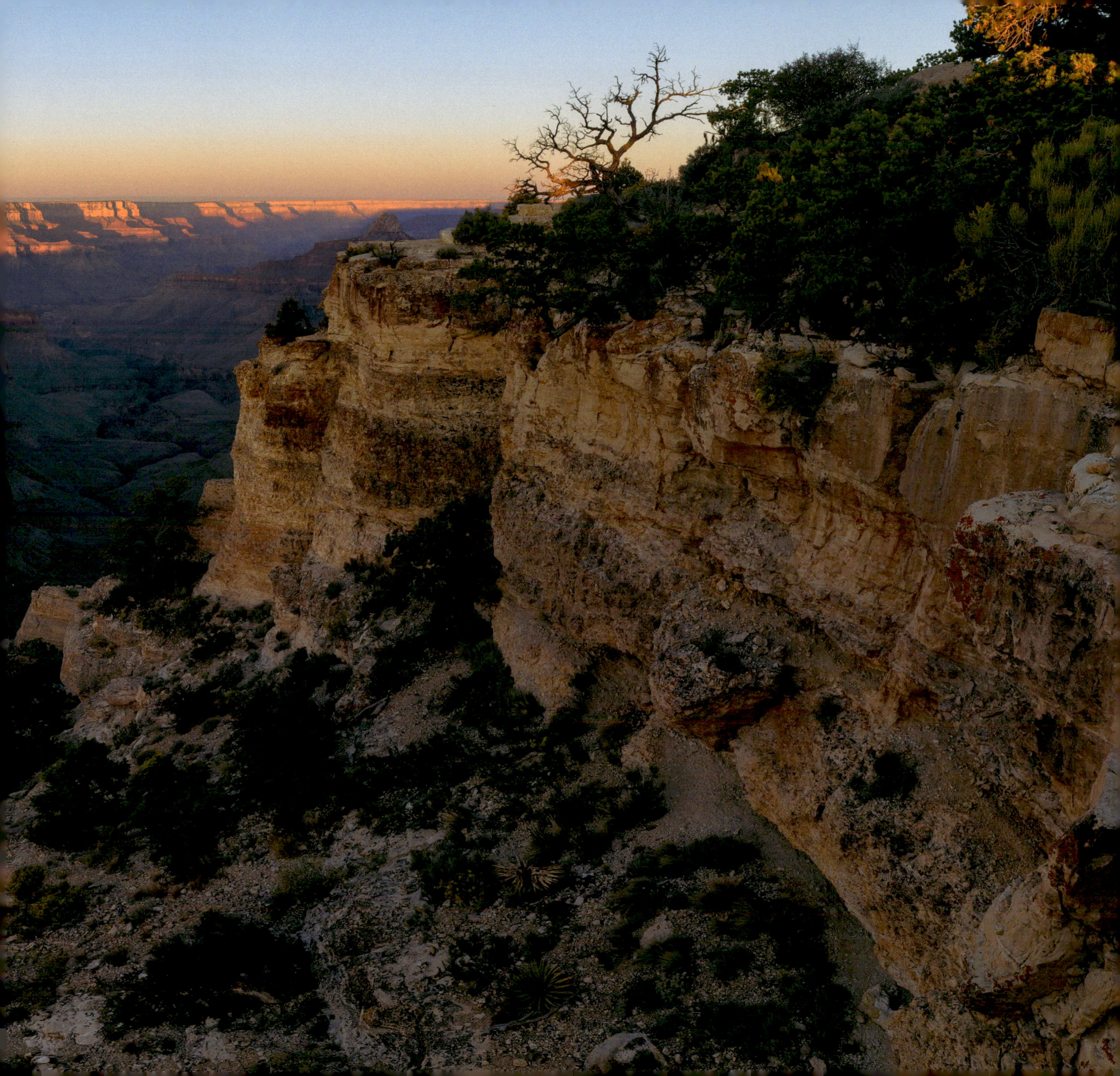

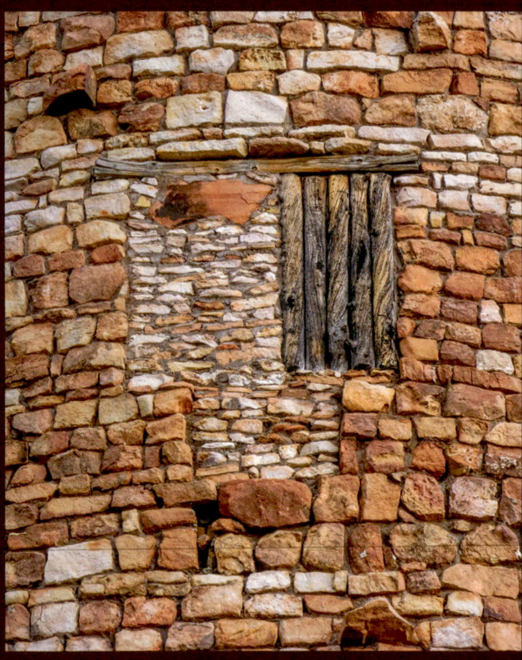

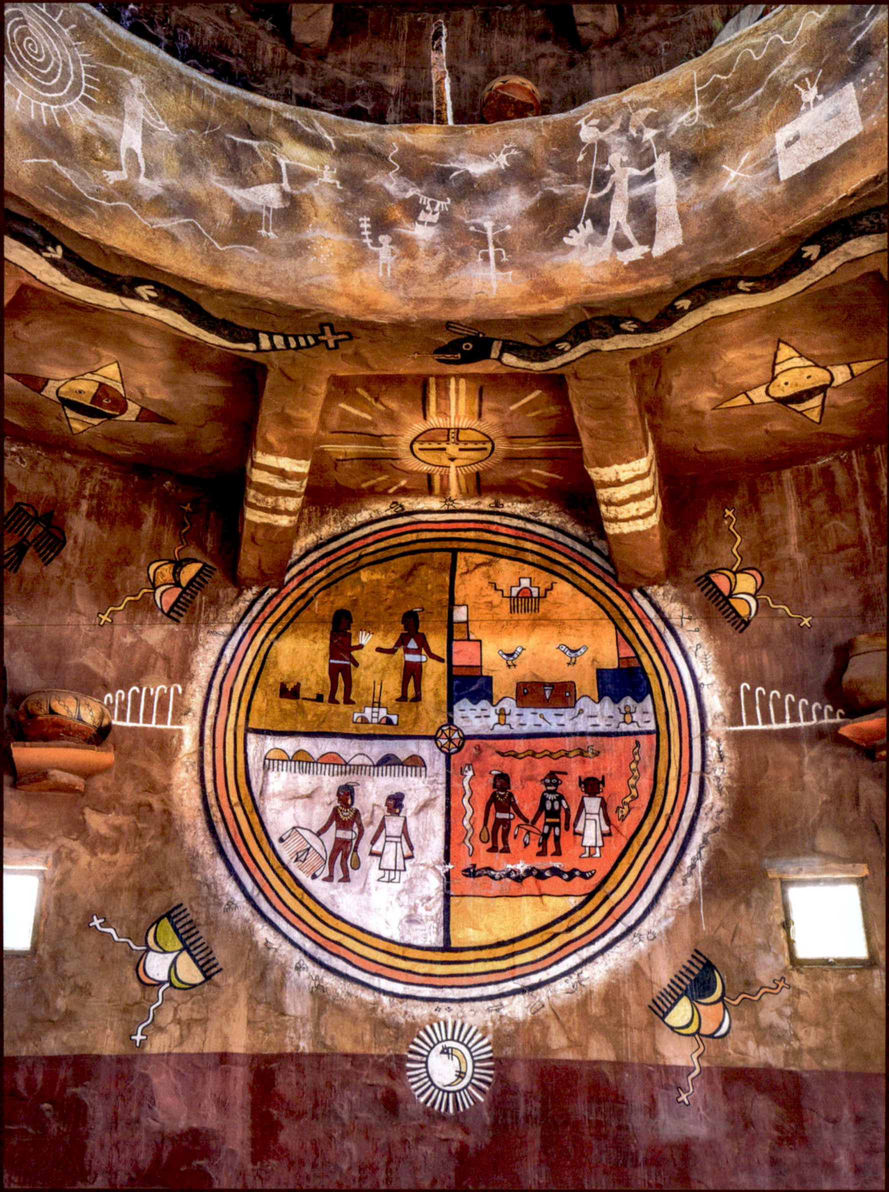

Above: A T-shaped doorway is filled in with stones and wood. Each exterior stone in the tower's walls was hand selected and placed.

Right: A mural on the Watchtower's first floor depicts the Hopi story of the first man to navigate the Colorado River, as painted by Hopi artist Fred Kabotie.

Facing page: Patterned after the architecture of Ancestral Puebloan towers, the Desert View Watchtower was built in 1932 and provides vistas from Marble Canyon in the north to the vast expanse of the Grand Canyon westward.

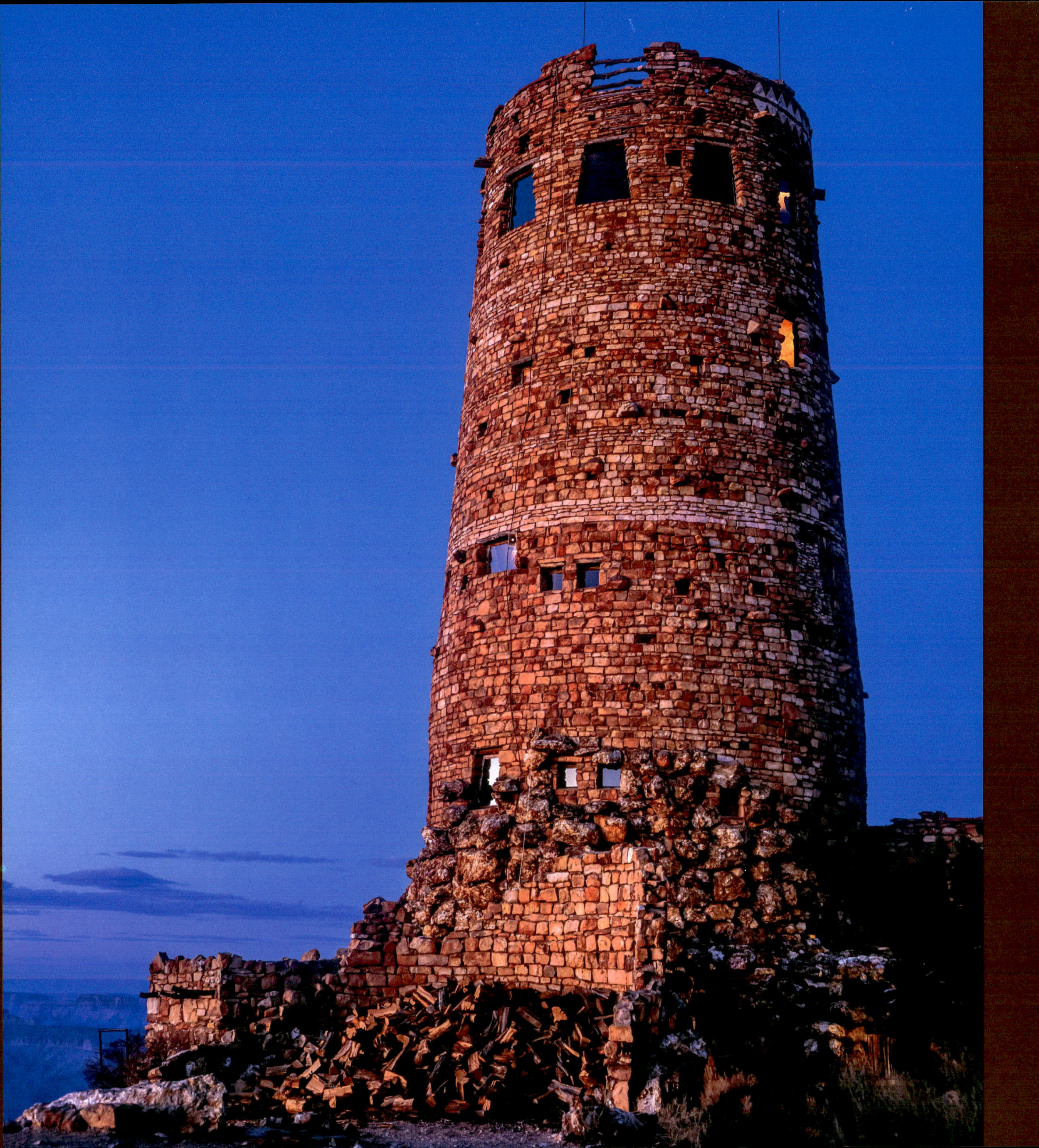

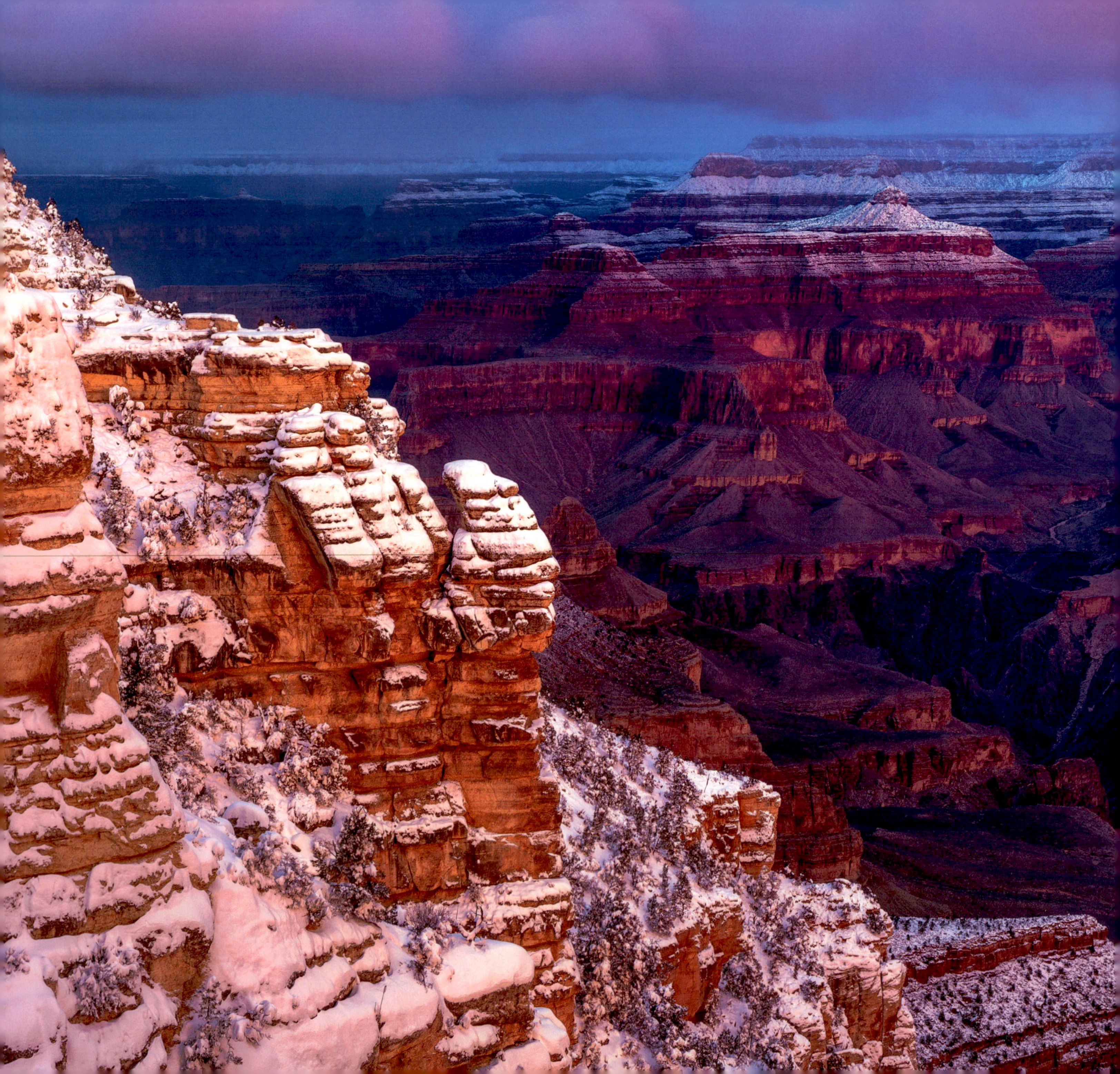

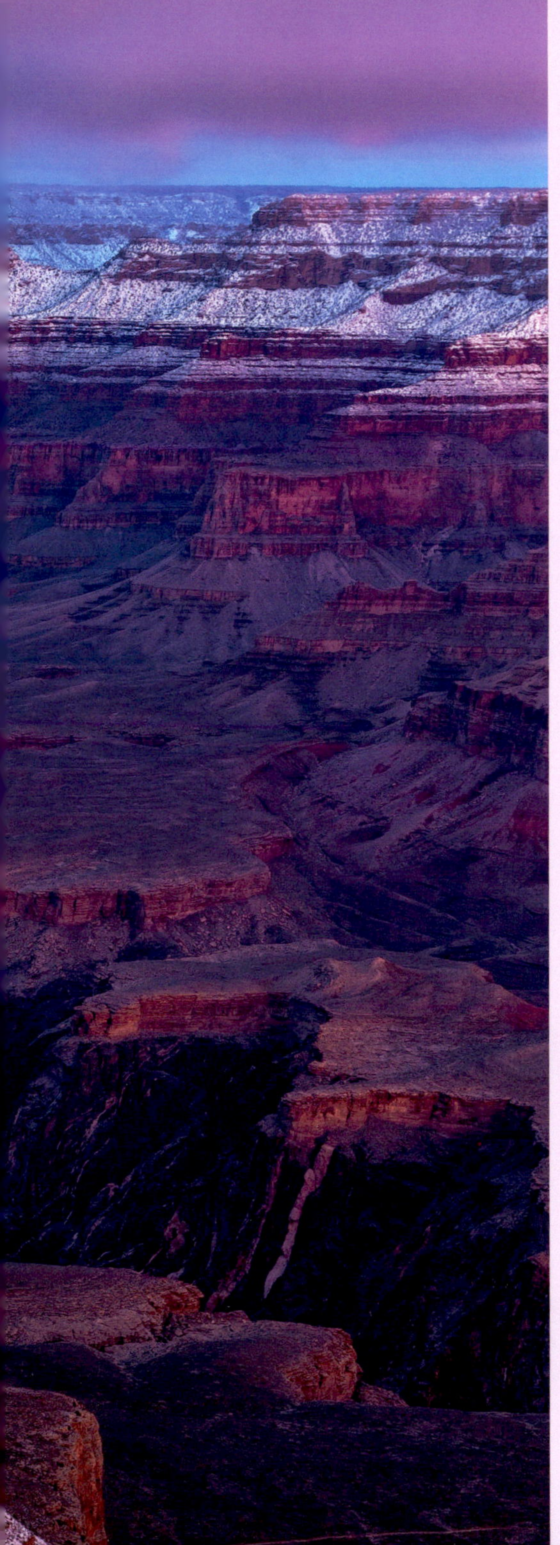

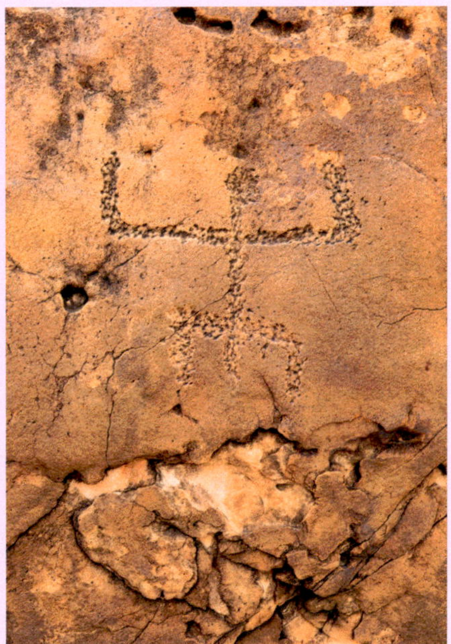

Left: A petroglyph of a man adorns a rocky bench above the mouth of South Canyon on the Colorado River.

Far left: Snow dusts the upper ledges of the Grand Canyon as seen from Mather Point on the South Rim.

Below: Prickly pear cactus flowers add a splash of vibrant color to the desert floor.

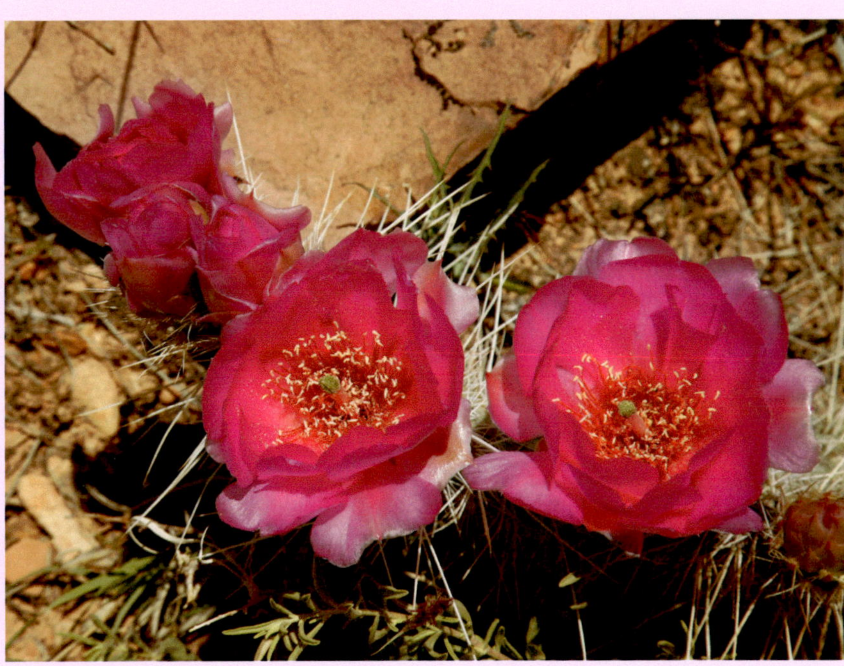

Right: A trailside thermometer registers 109 degrees Fahrenheit on the Bright Angel Trail. Hikers are advised to start early in the day and carry ample water.

Far right: The Colorado River churns through Granite Rapids, which are accessible on foot from the South Rim via the Monument Creek Trail.

Below: The main chute at Granite Rapids draws river runners close to the wall of the north bank for an exciting ride.

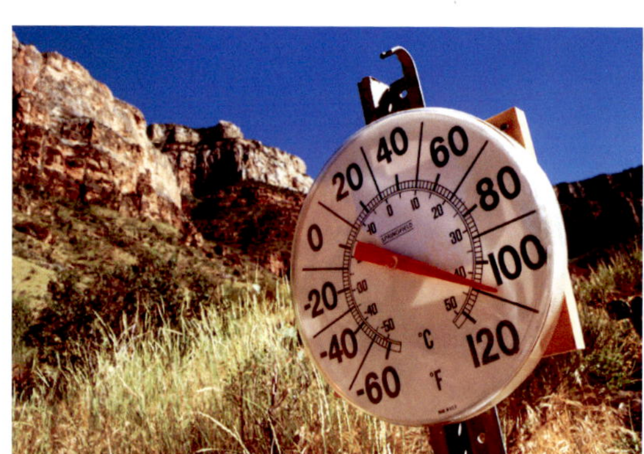

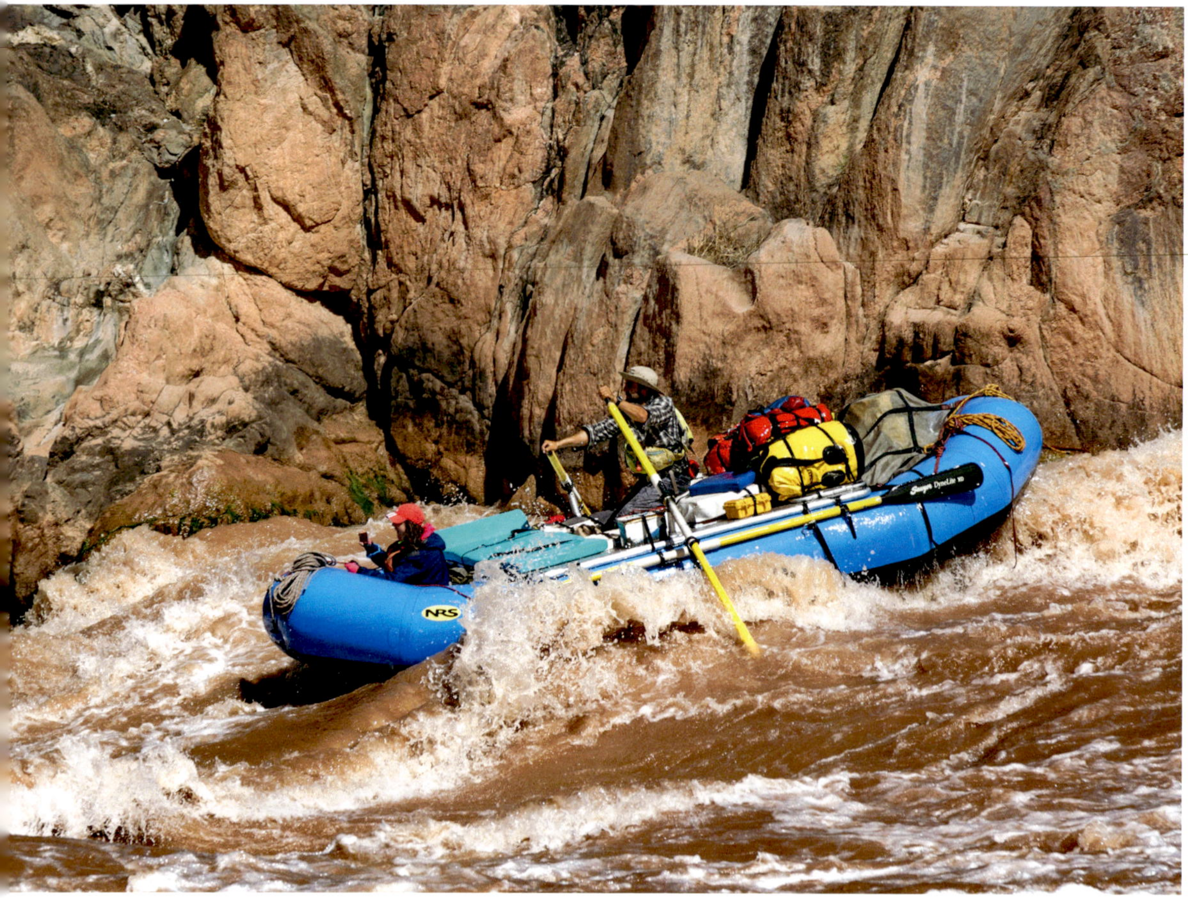

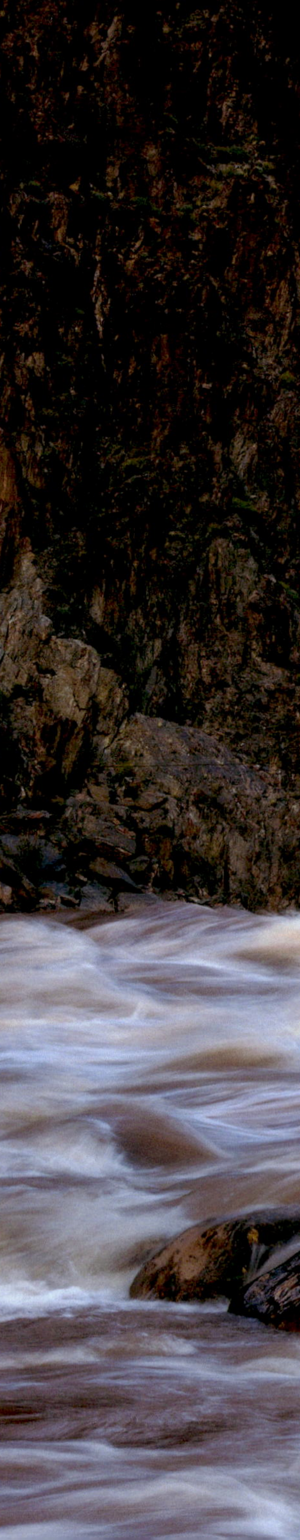

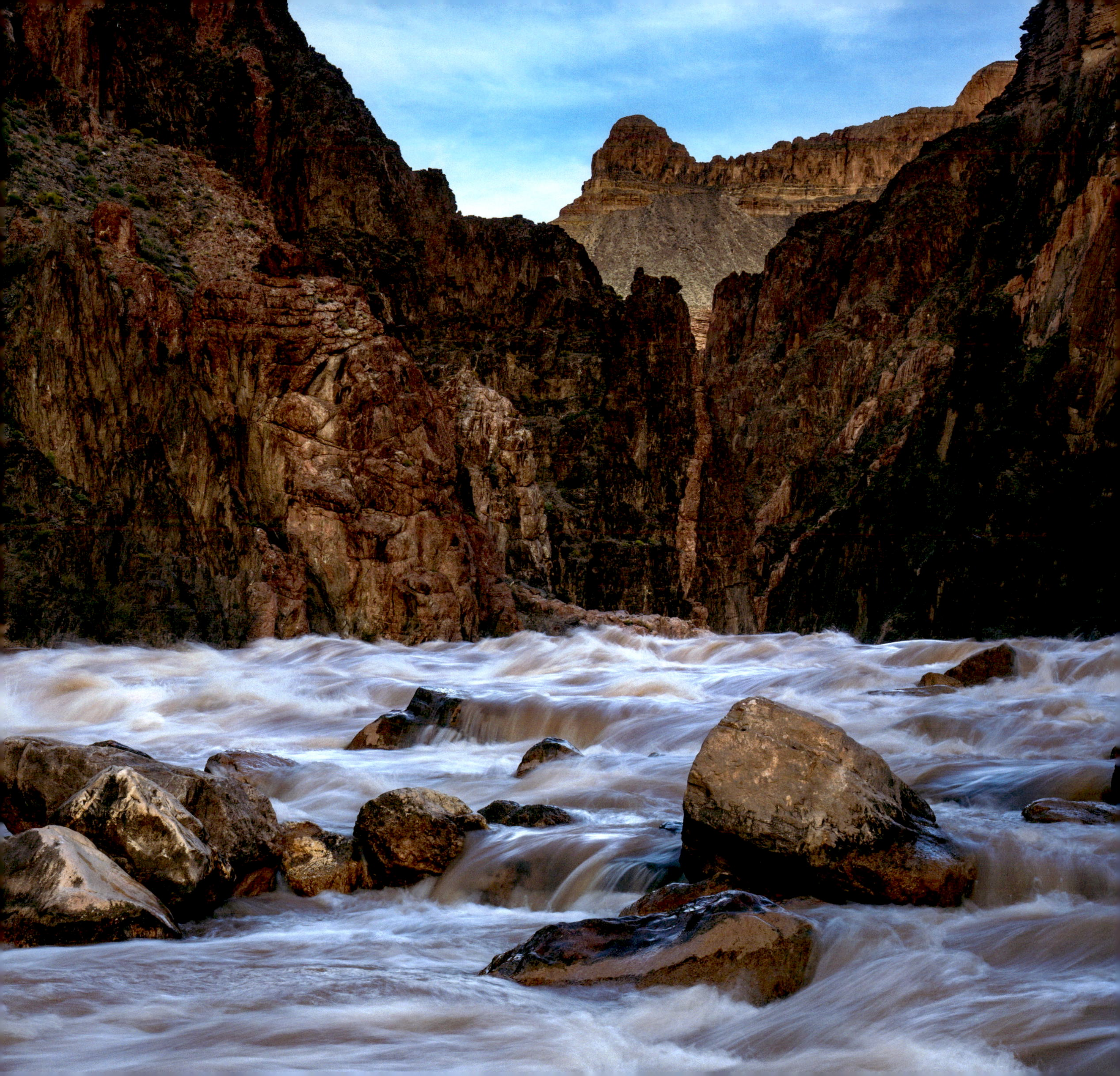

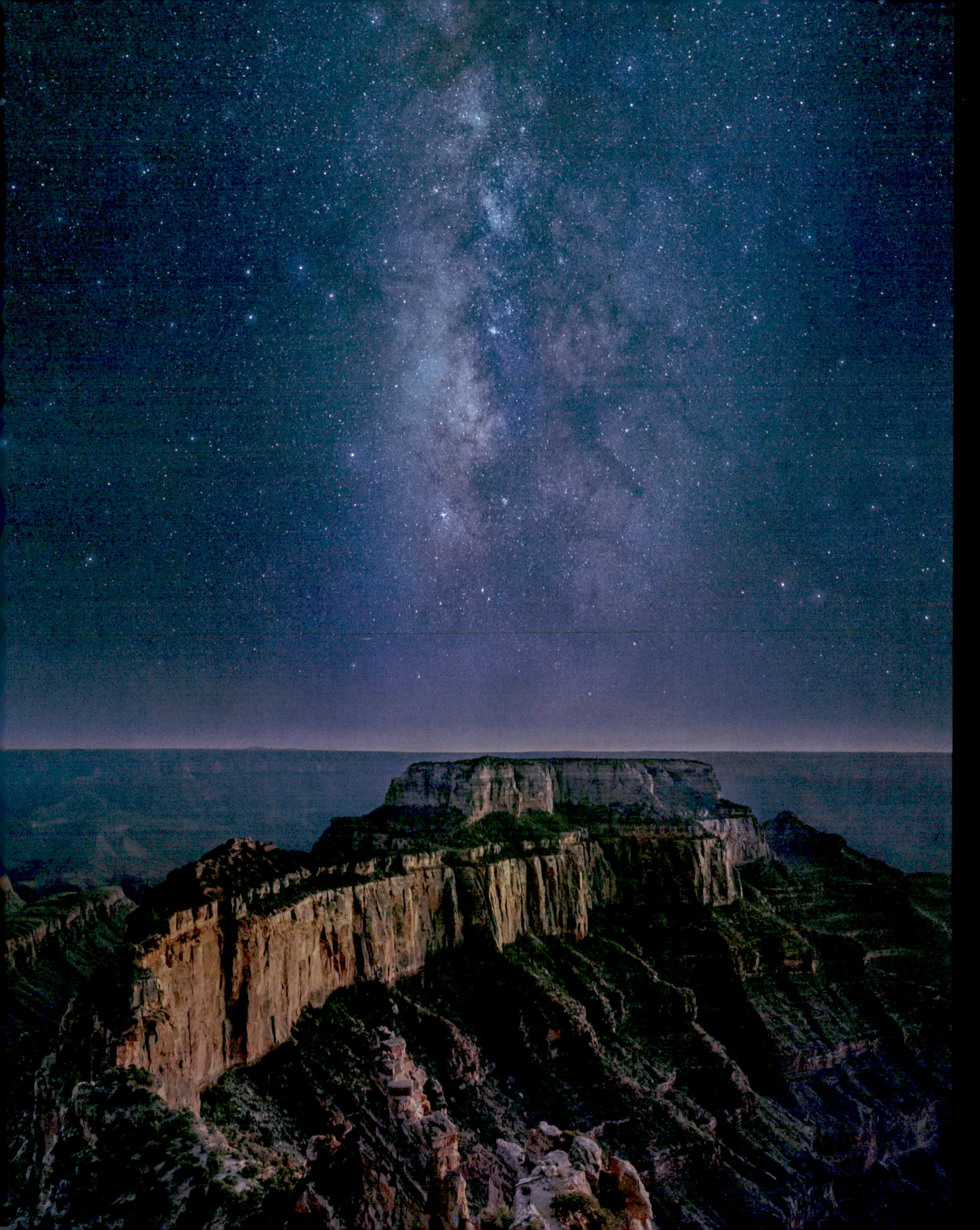

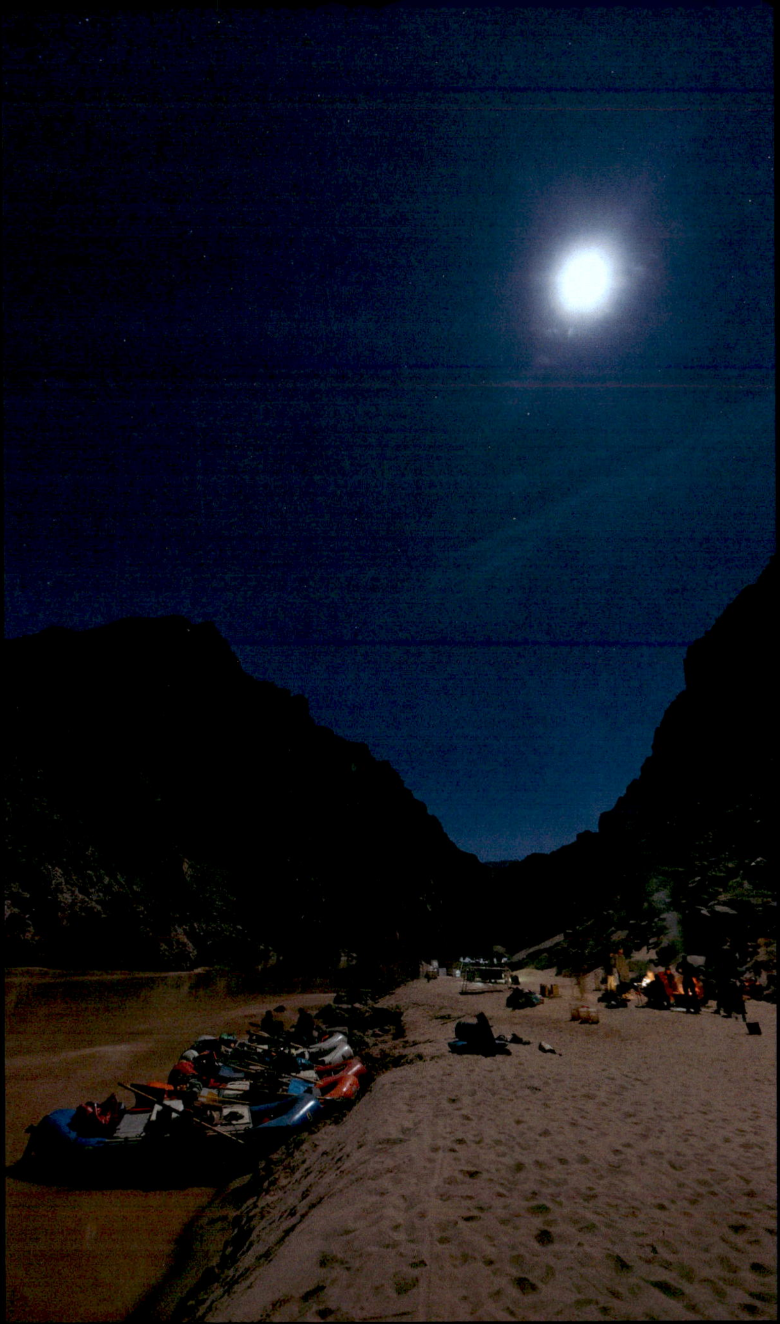

Left: A full moon illuminates Grapevine Camp across from the mouth of Vishnu Creek and just upstream from Grapevine Rapids.

Facing page: The Milky Way soars above the ramparts of Wotans Throne.

Below: Lodging options at the North Rim include these rustic but comfortable cabins at Grand Canyon Lodge.

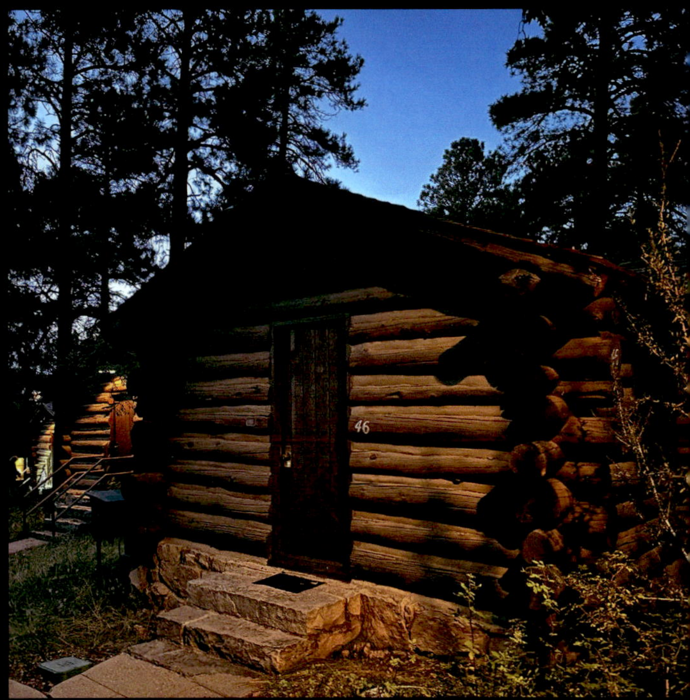

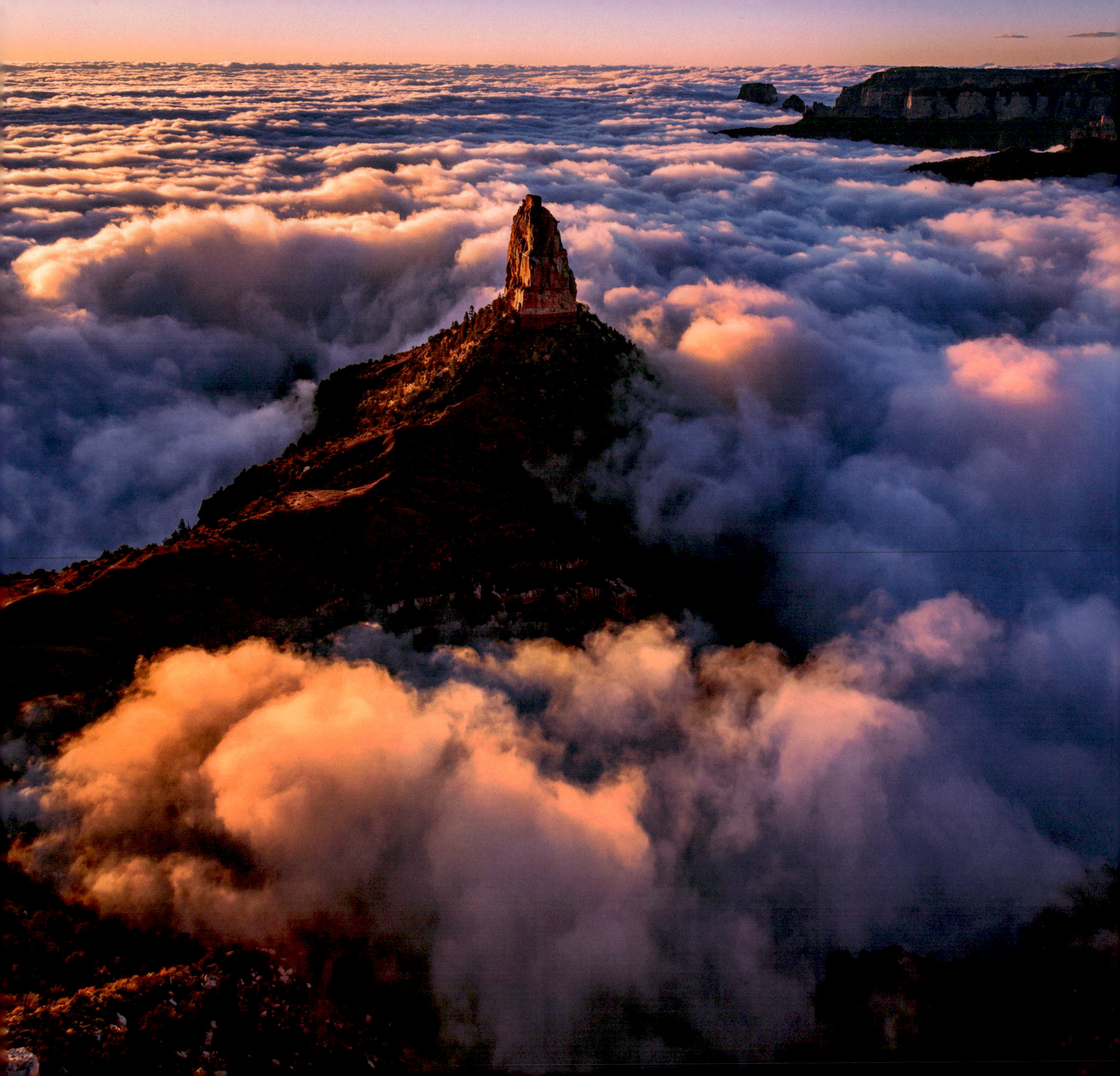

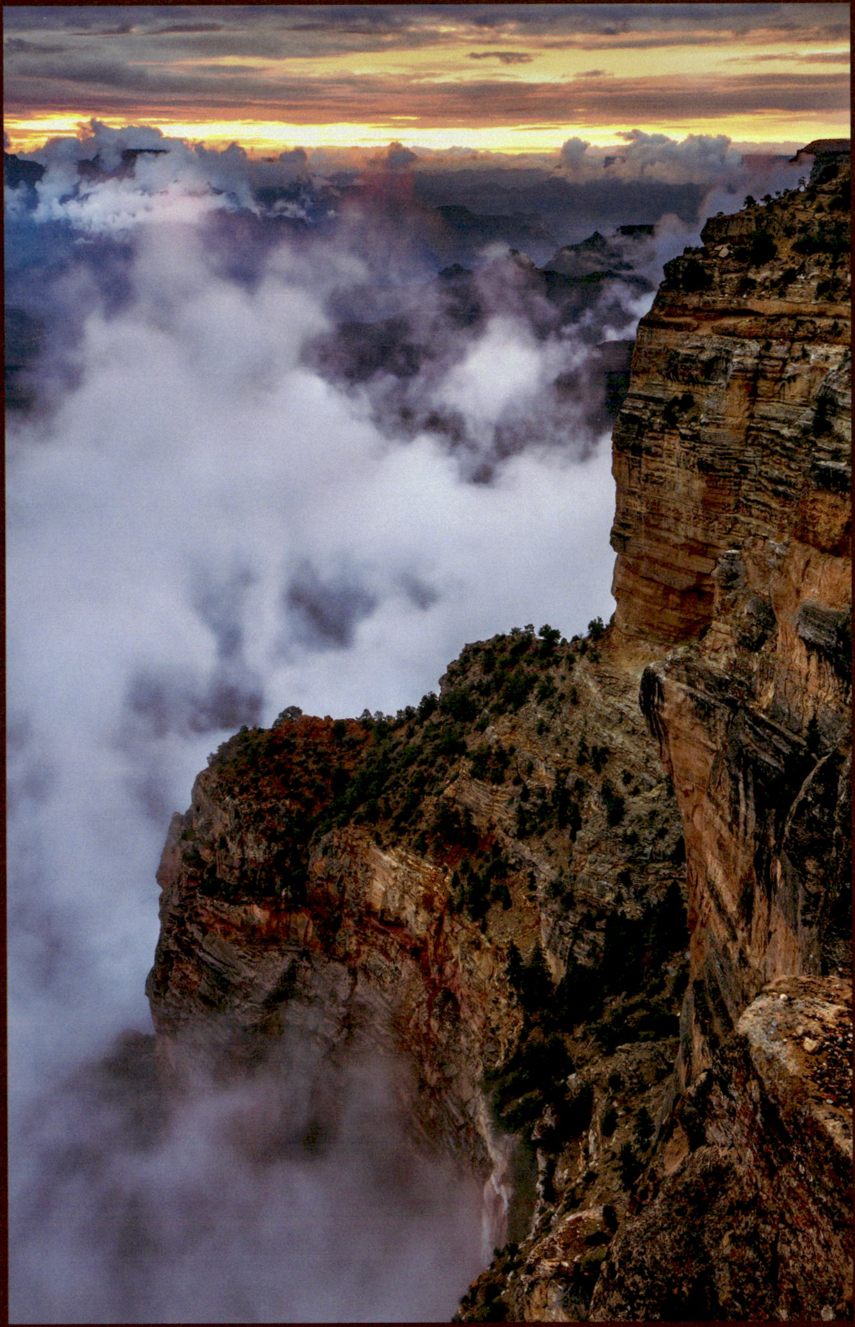

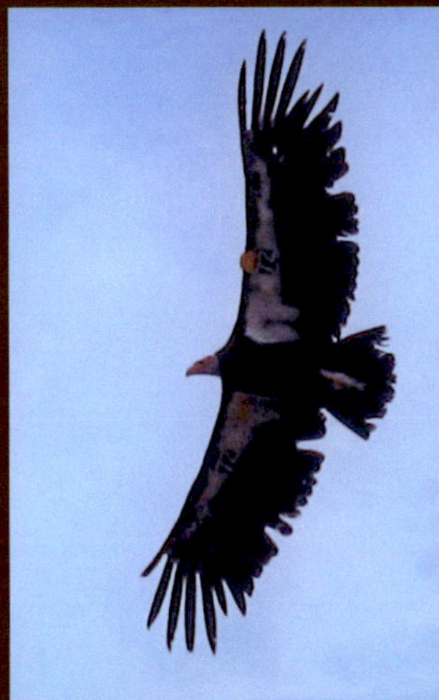

Above: Perhaps the world's rarest birds, California condors had dwindled to just 22 individuals by 1982. A captive breeding program and releases into the wild have successfully returned condors to Arizona skies.

Left: Low clouds hunker below daybreak at Hopi Point on the South Rim.

Far left: At sunrise, the spire of Mount Hayden catches sunrise above a thick blanket of clouds, as seen from Point Imperial on the North Rim.

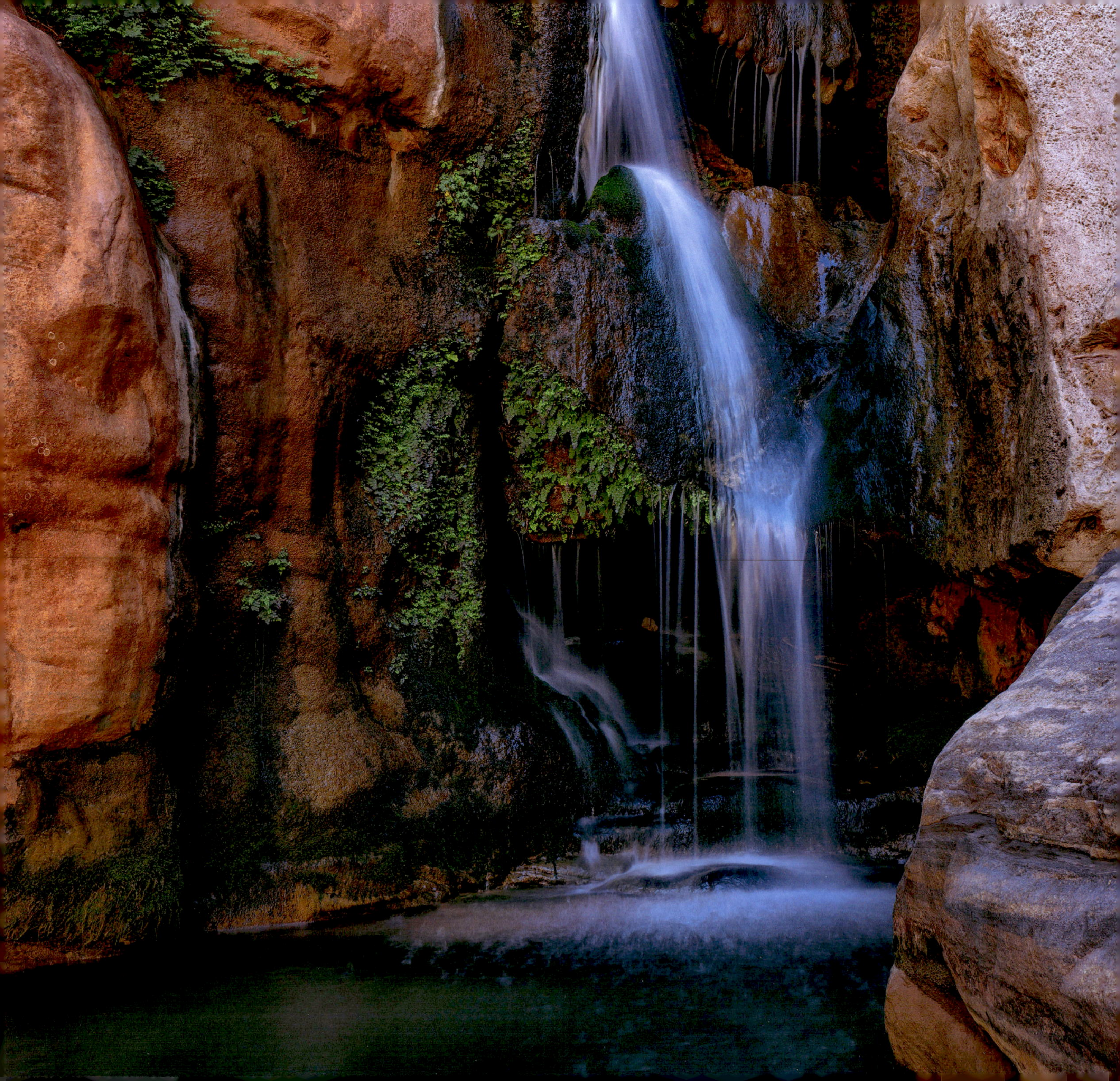

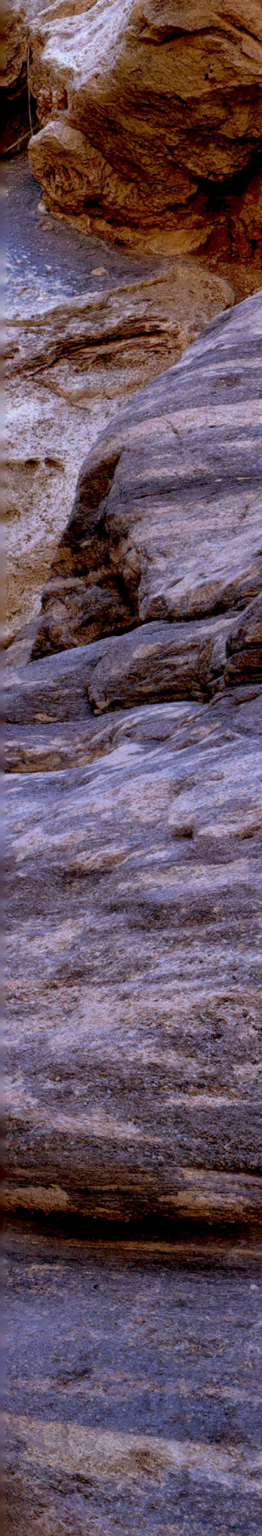

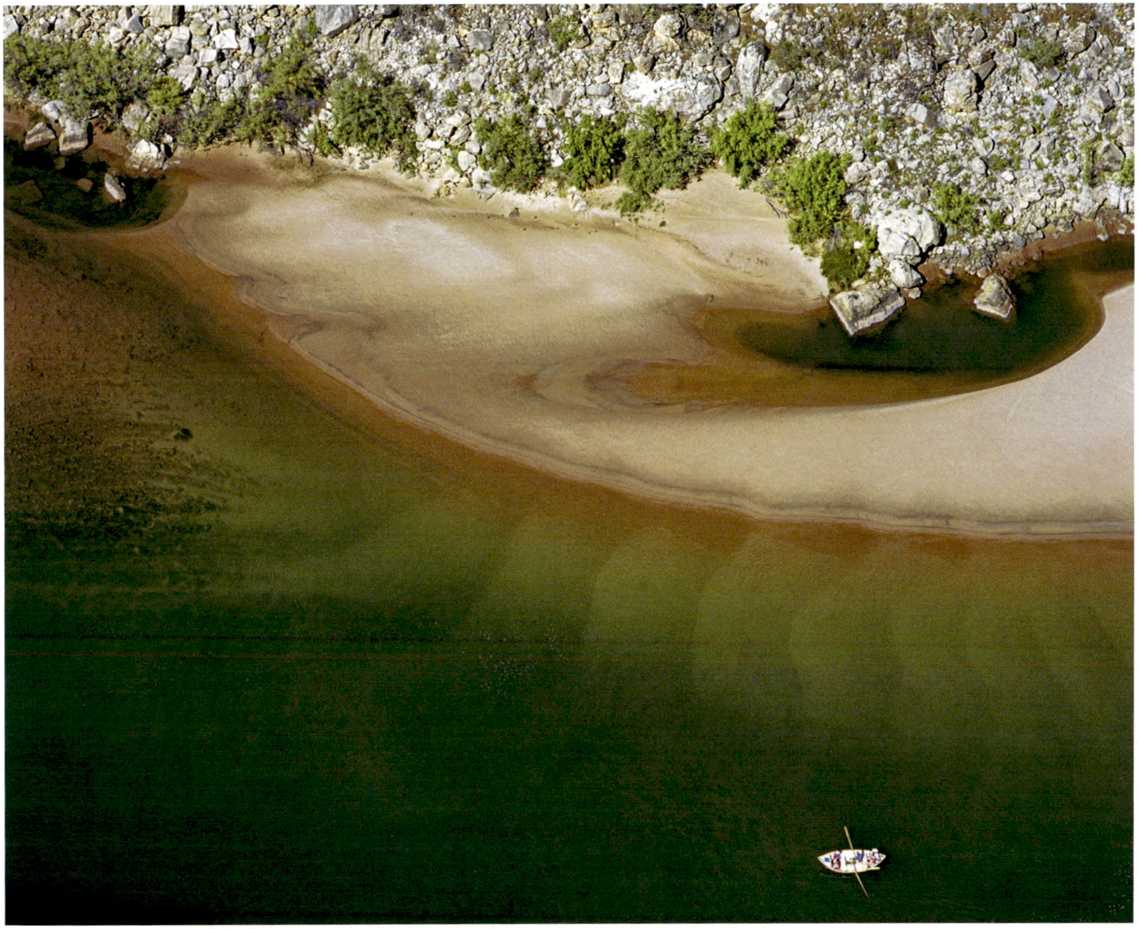

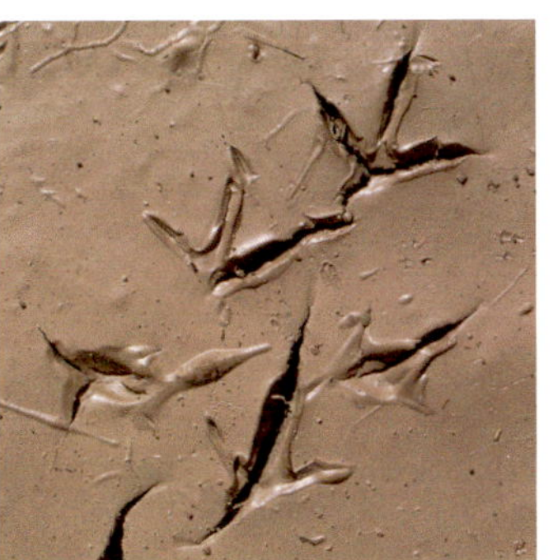

Above: A wooden dory floats above streambed ripples on the clear upper reach of the Colorado River.

Left: Shoreline mud holds the tracks of a great blue heron on the Little Colorado River above the confluence with the main Colorado.

Far left: An intimate grotto known as Elves Chasm nestles a few hundred feet above the Colorado River on Royal Arch Creek.

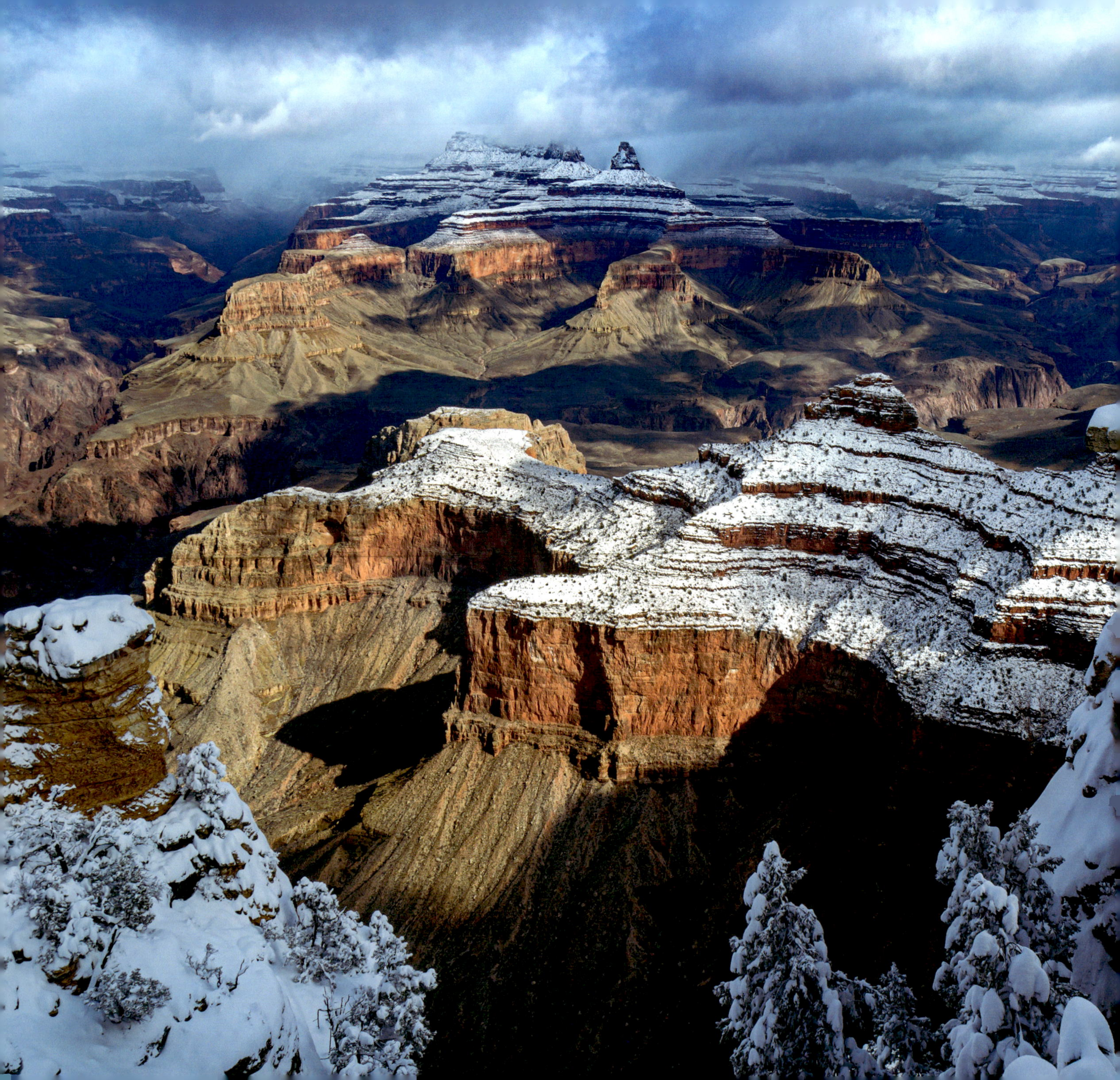

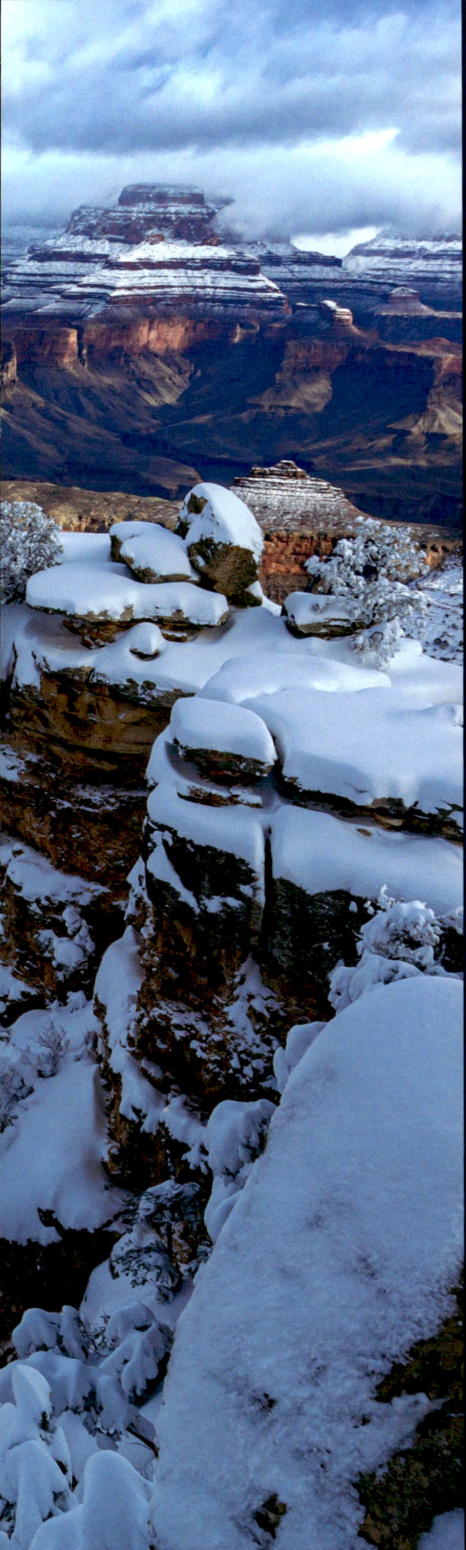

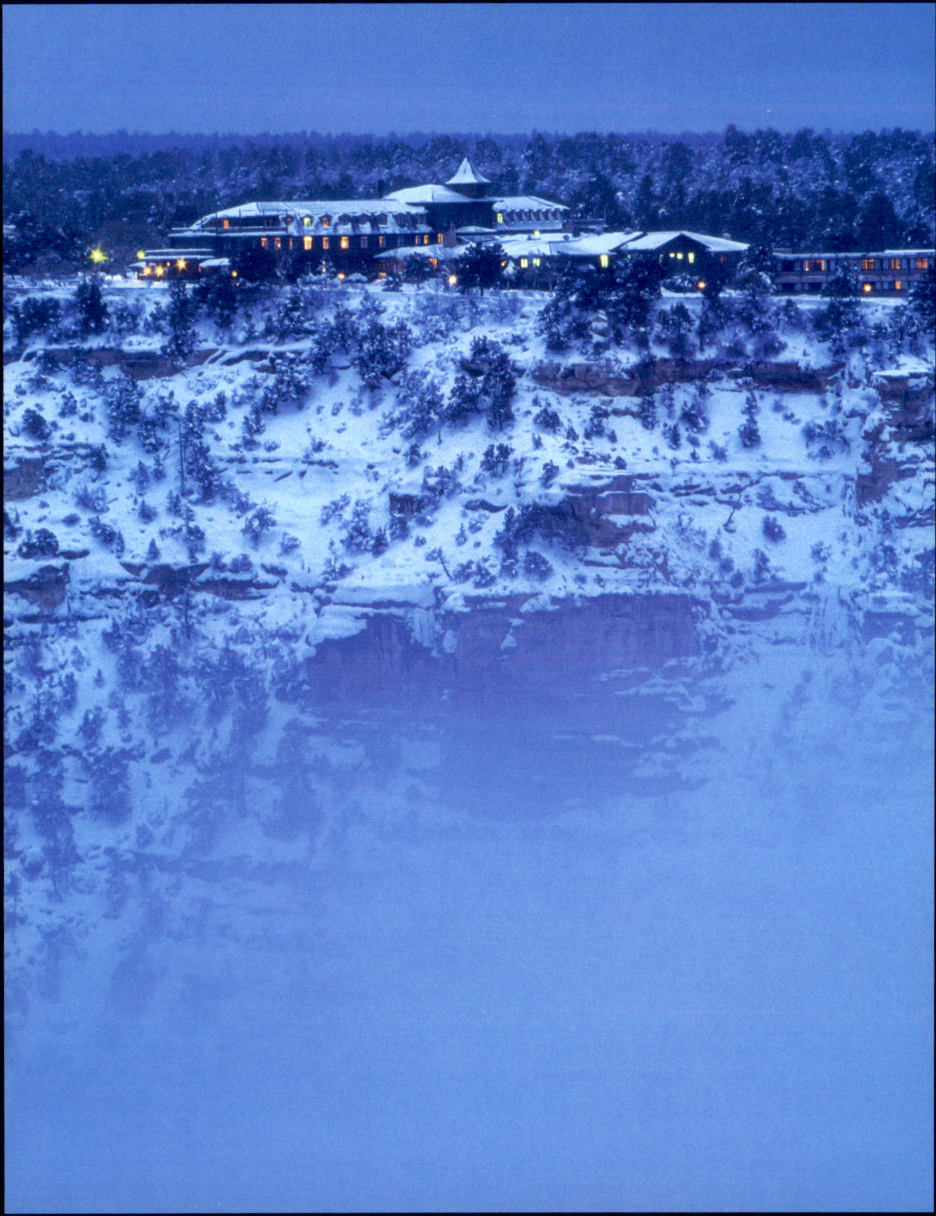

Above: El Tovar glows warmly against the snow and fog of a winter's day on the South Rim.

Left: A passing winter storm adds a layer of white to the Grand Canyon's banded formations.

Right: Some 2,000 to 4,000 years ago, someone left this split-twig figurine in a cave among the walls of the Grand Canyon.

Far right: High on a cliff face above the Colorado River, one of a series of ancient granaries above the Nankoweap Delta once sheltered corn and other foods from the elements.

Below: Rich in iron, red pictographs below the South Rim reveal a snapshot of the Grand Canyon's rich prehistoric heritage.

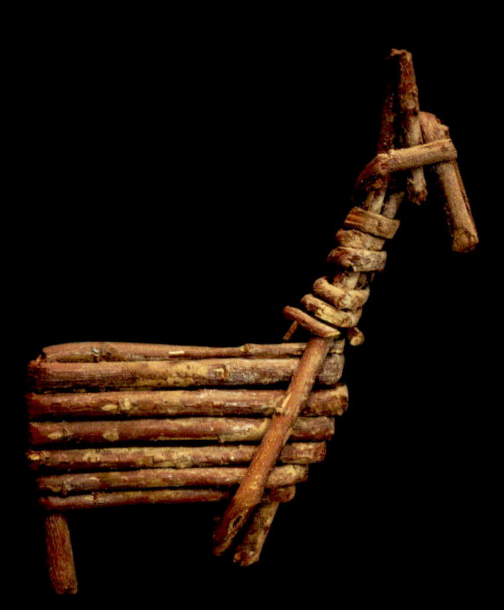

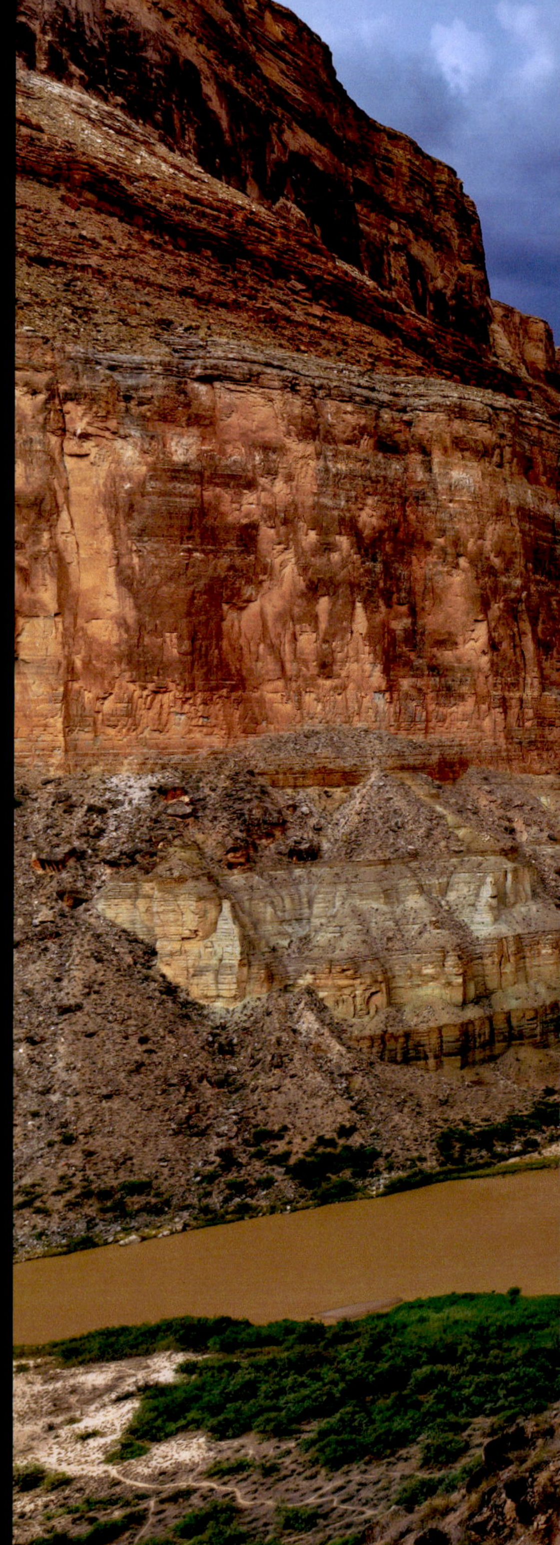

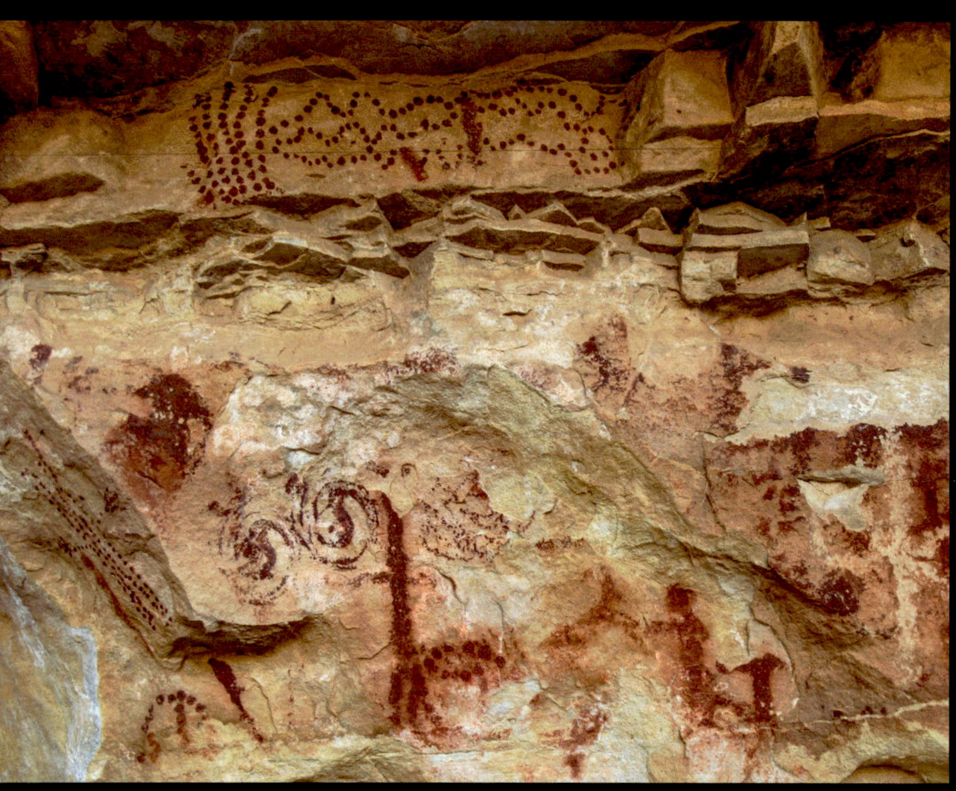

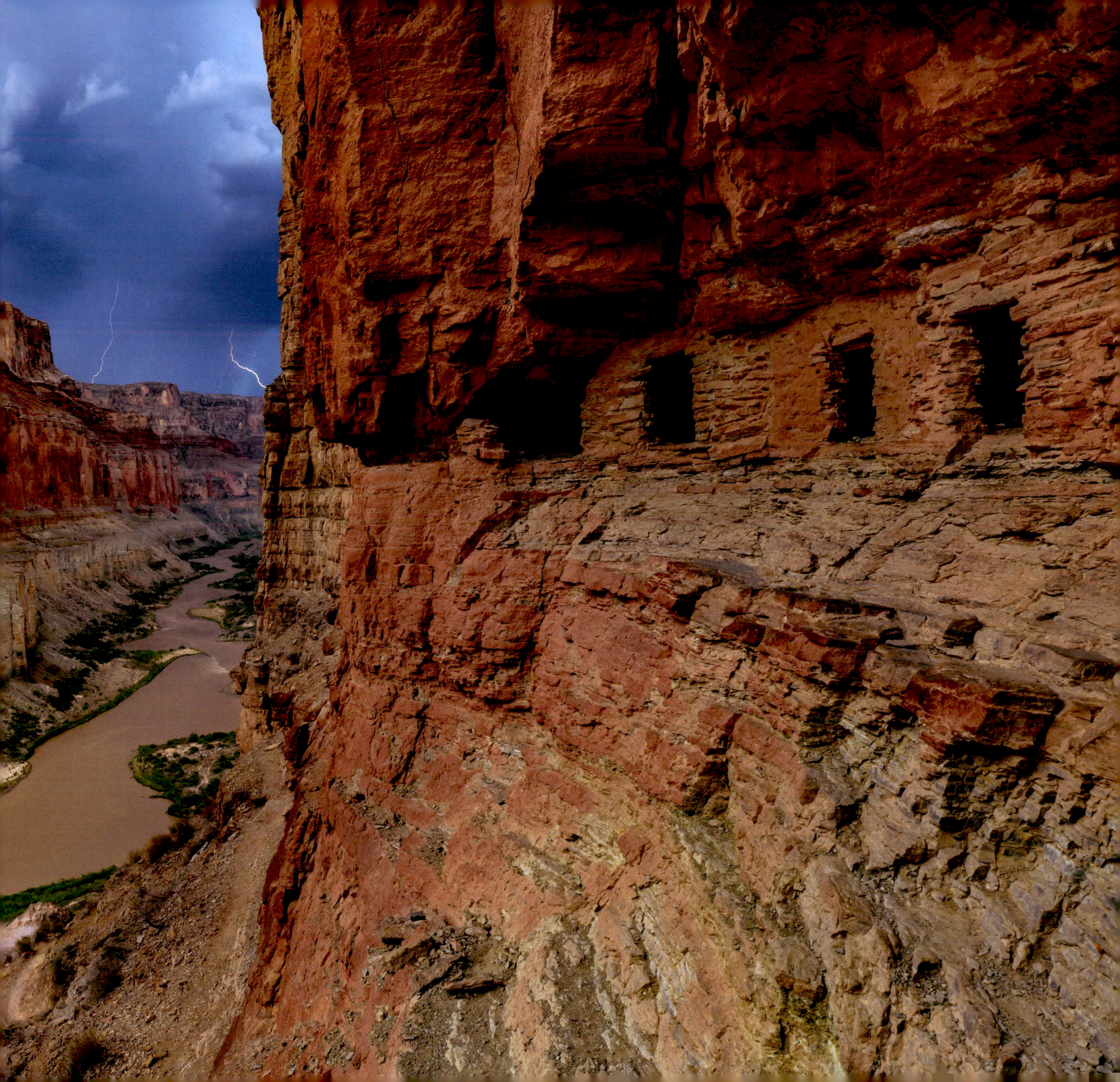

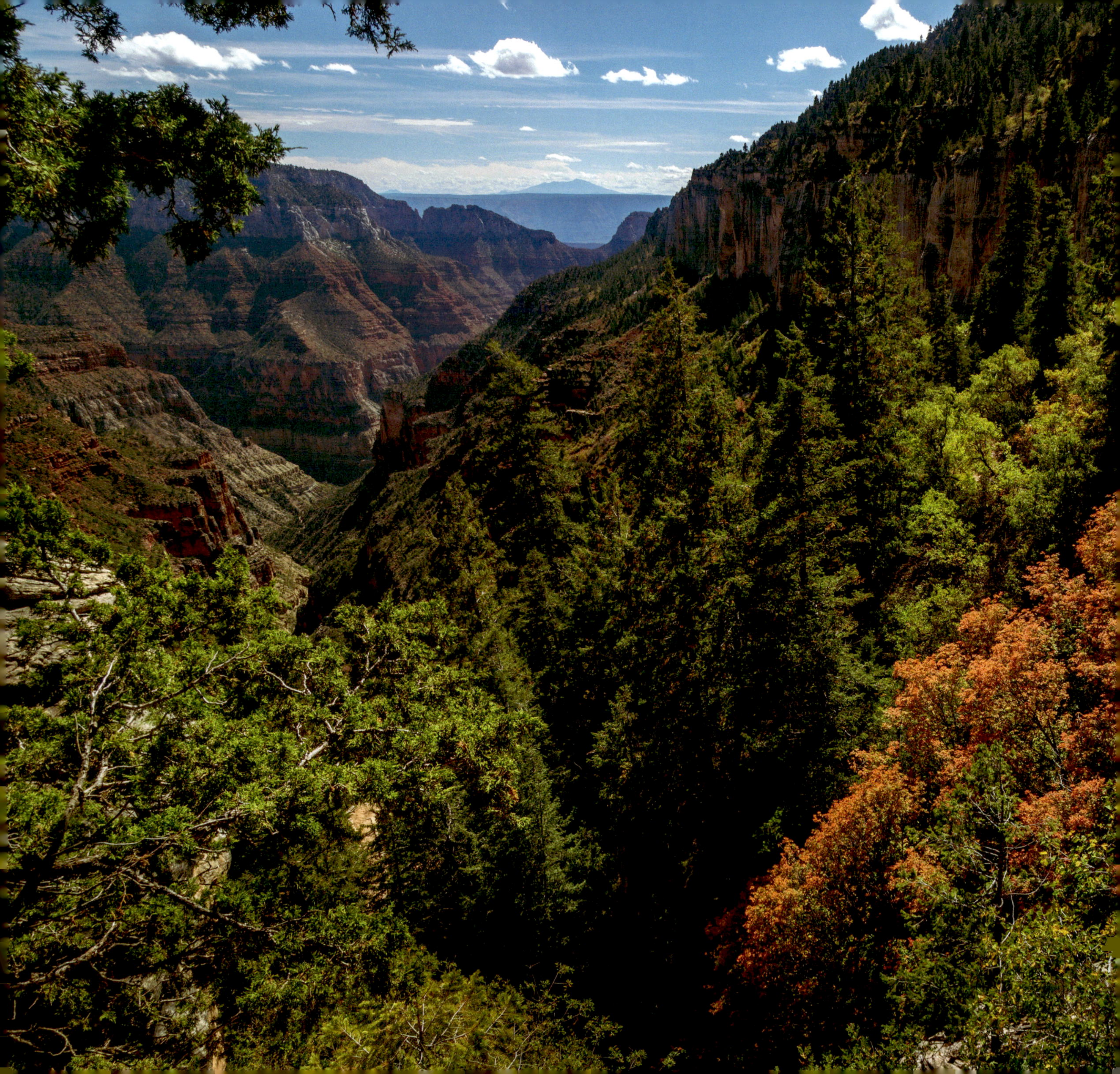

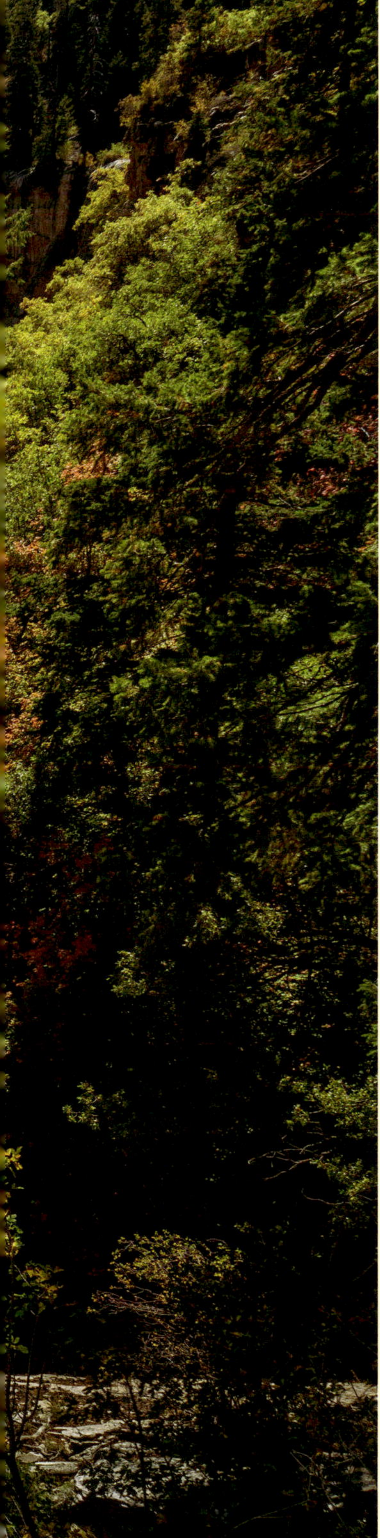

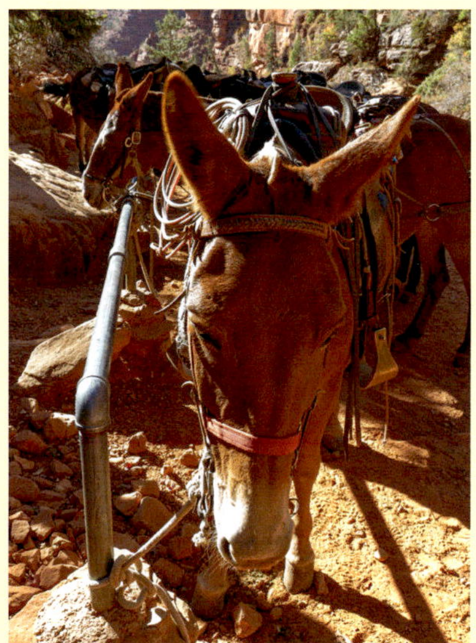

Left: Sure-footed mules remain a popular way to experience the Grand Canyon, with several guided options from both the North and South Rims.

Far left: Autumn colors arrive early at Coconino Overlook on the North Kaibab Trail.

Below: Mules rest at Havasupai Gardens, a midway point along the Bright Angel Trail from the South Rim.

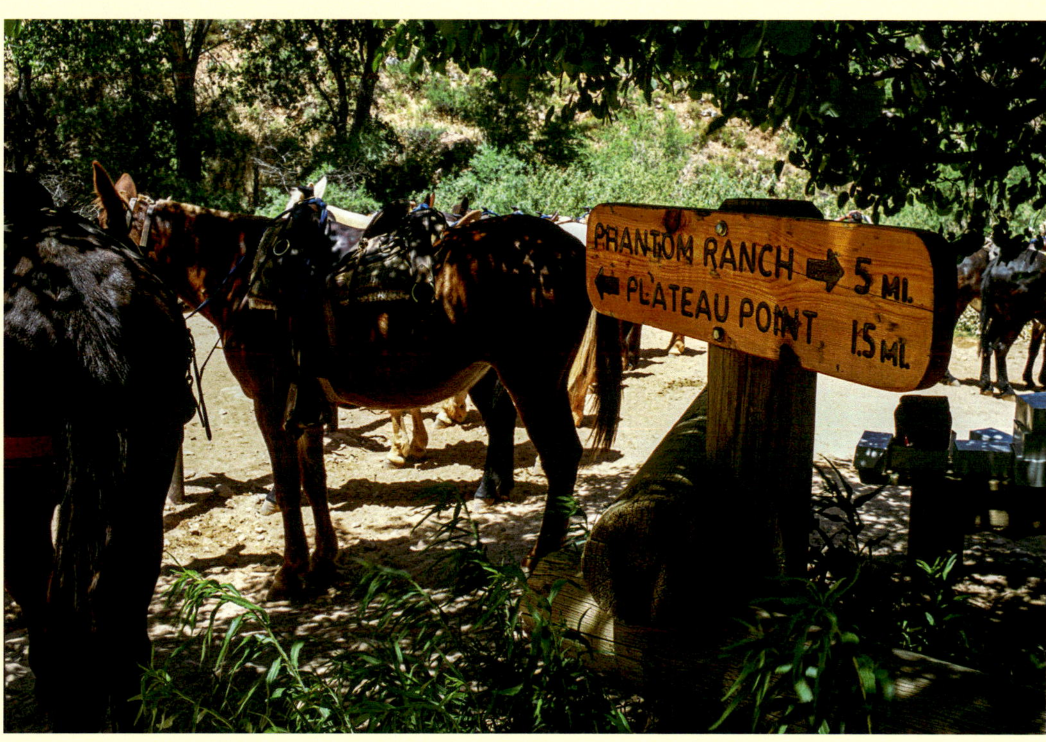

Right: Periodic floods and natural erosion continue to change the configuration of Havasu Falls. The plunge pool and surrounding canyon are an idyllic oasis on Havasupai tribal lands south of Grand Canyon National Park.

Below: High concentrations of calcium carbonate and reflected blue skies result in the blue-green hues of lower Havasu Creek.

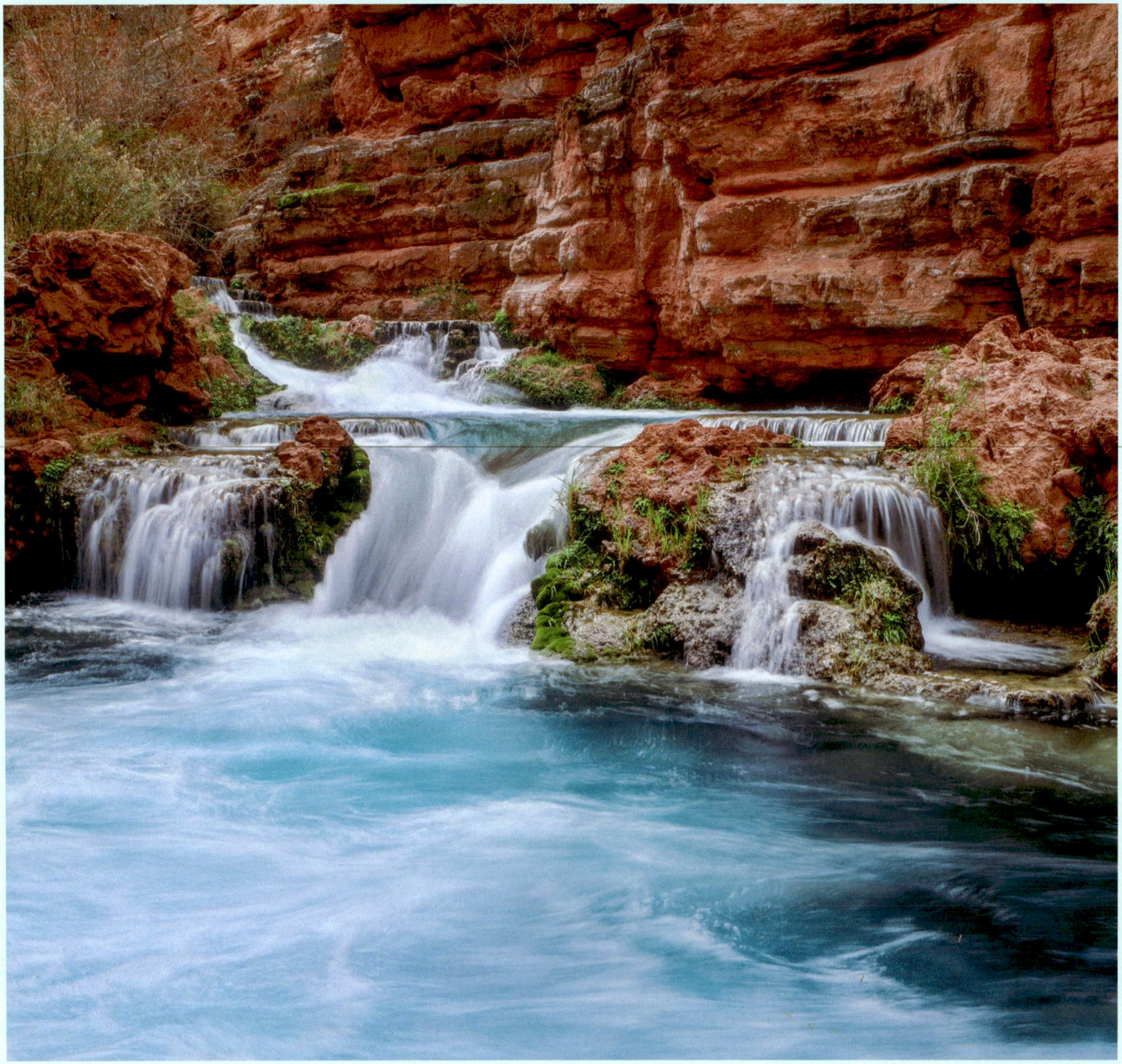

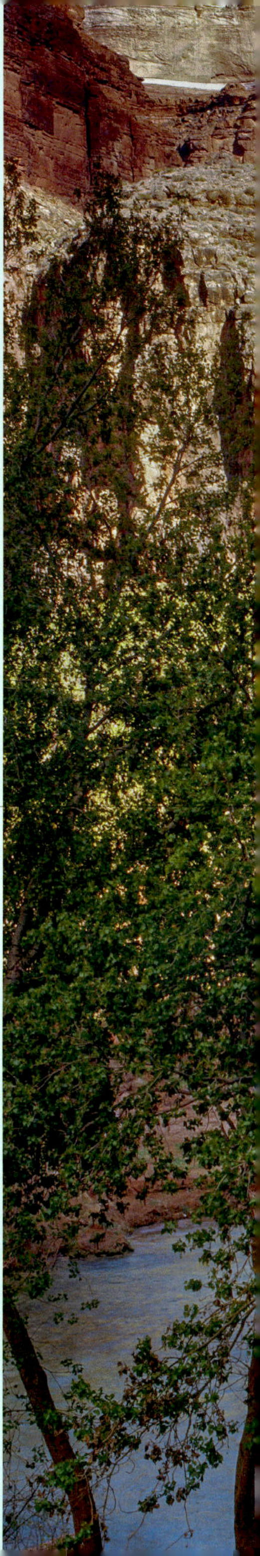

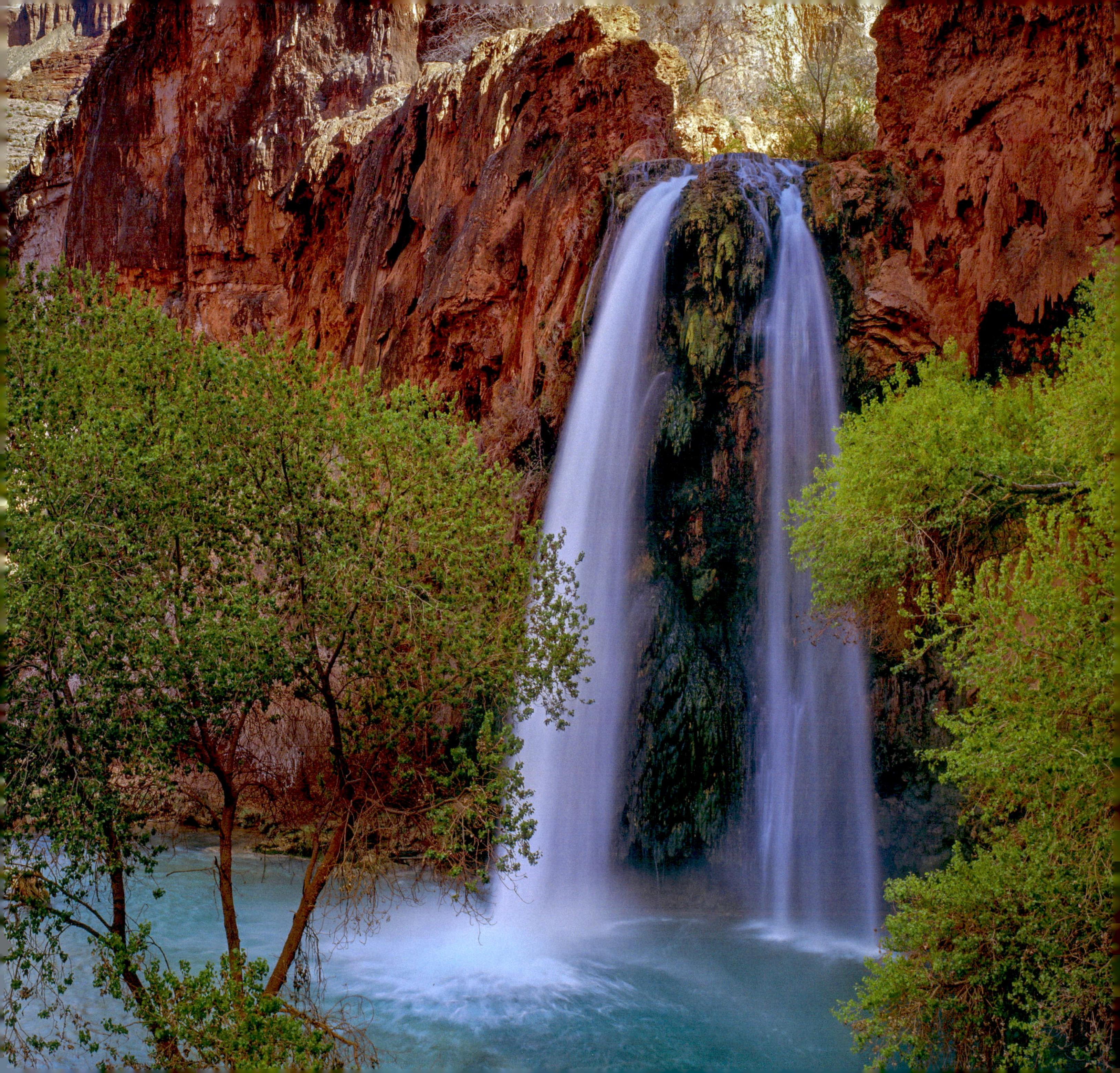

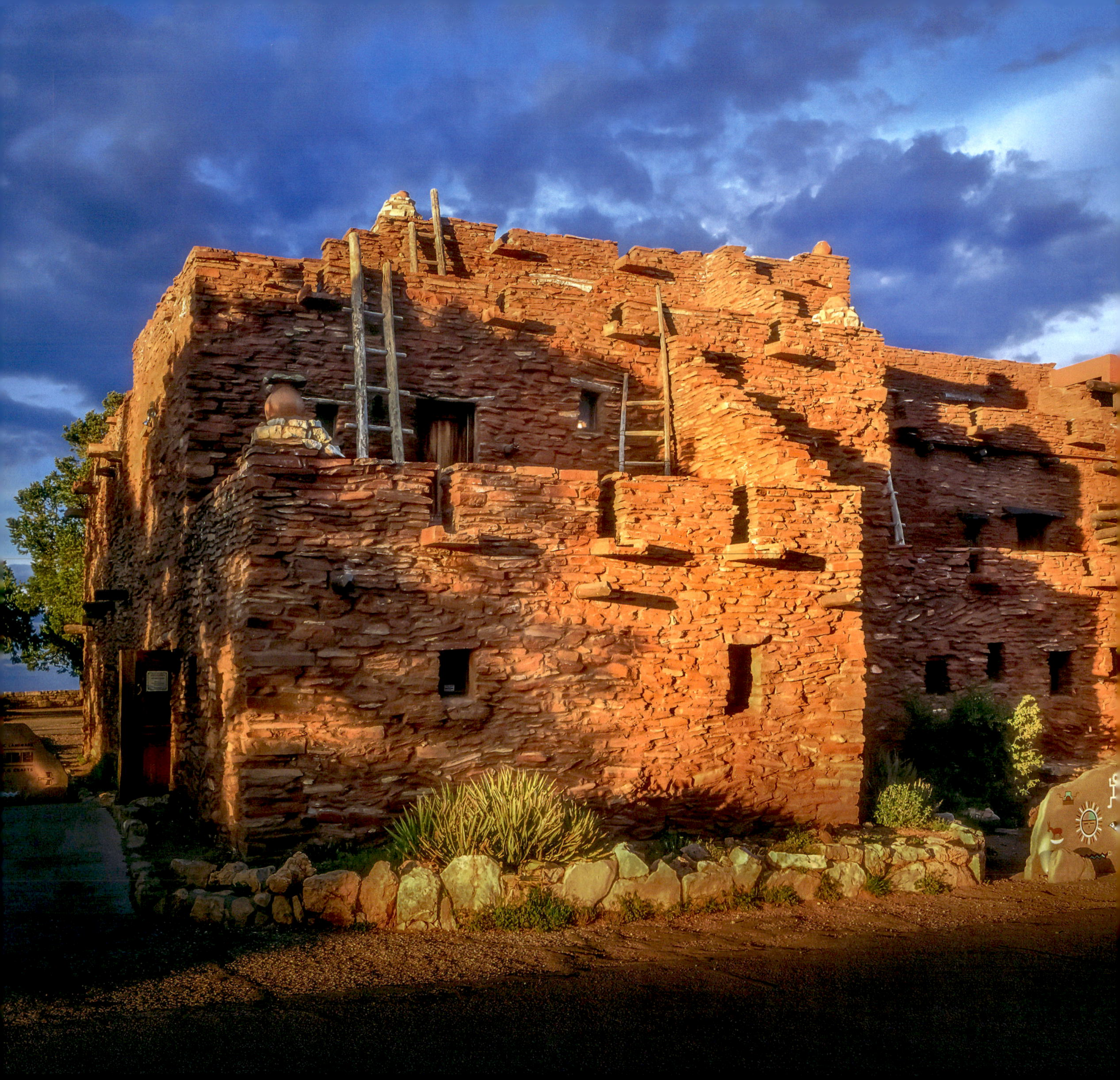

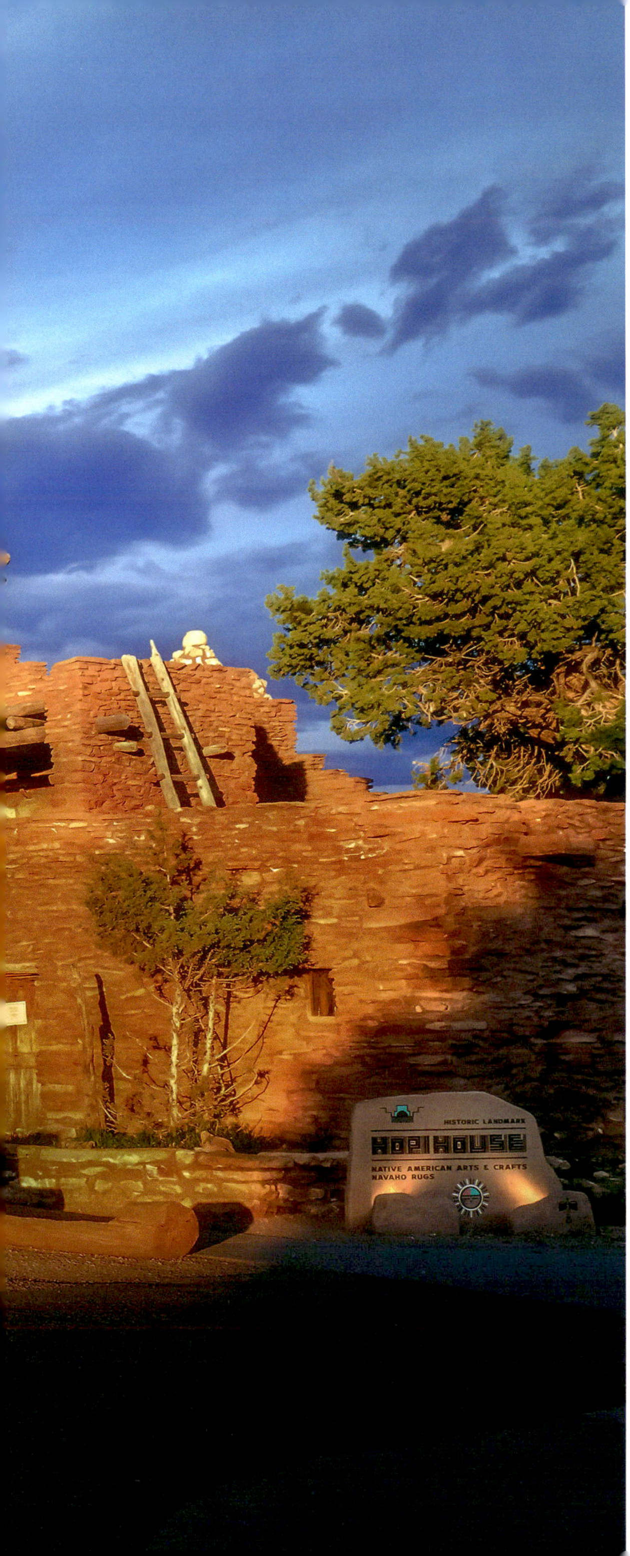

Left: Mary Colter styled Hopi House (a gift shop at Grand Canyon Village on the South Rim) after Hopi pueblo architecture. Completed in 1905, much of the construction was done by Hopi workers, and tribal artisans demonstrated their pottery, weaving, and jewelry-making here.

Following pages: In such a grand landscape, weather and light conspire to create constant change.

Below: A self-guiding trail loops around Tusayan Pueblo, remains of an Ancestral Puebloan village, on Desert View Drive.

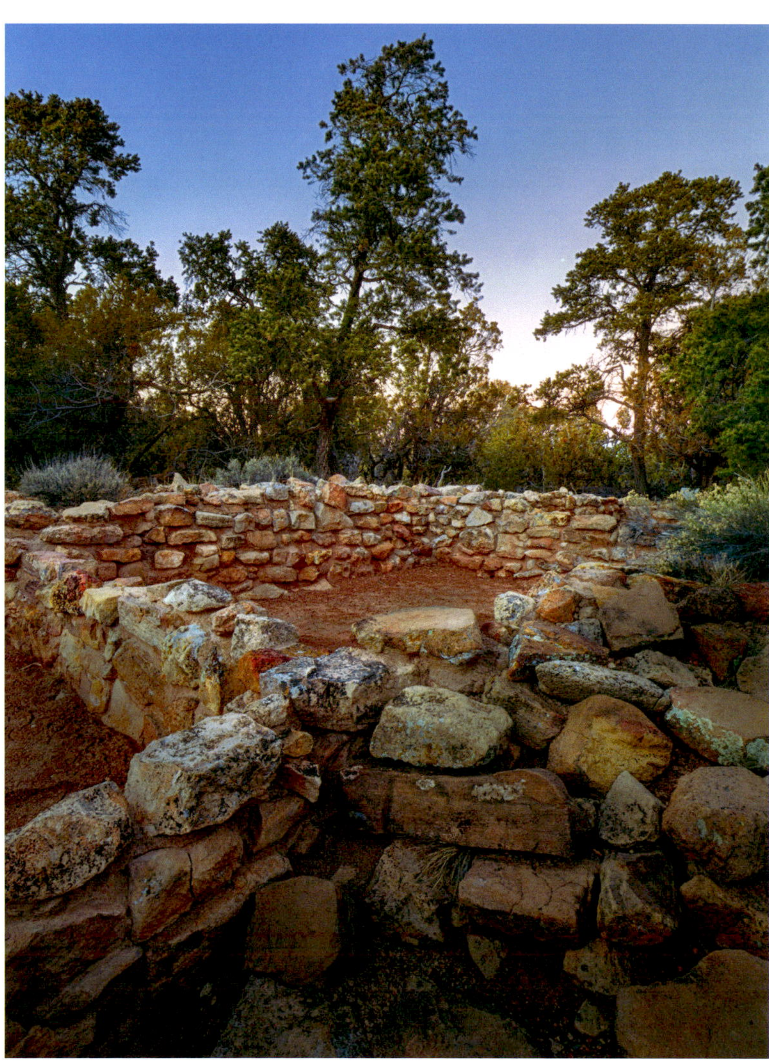

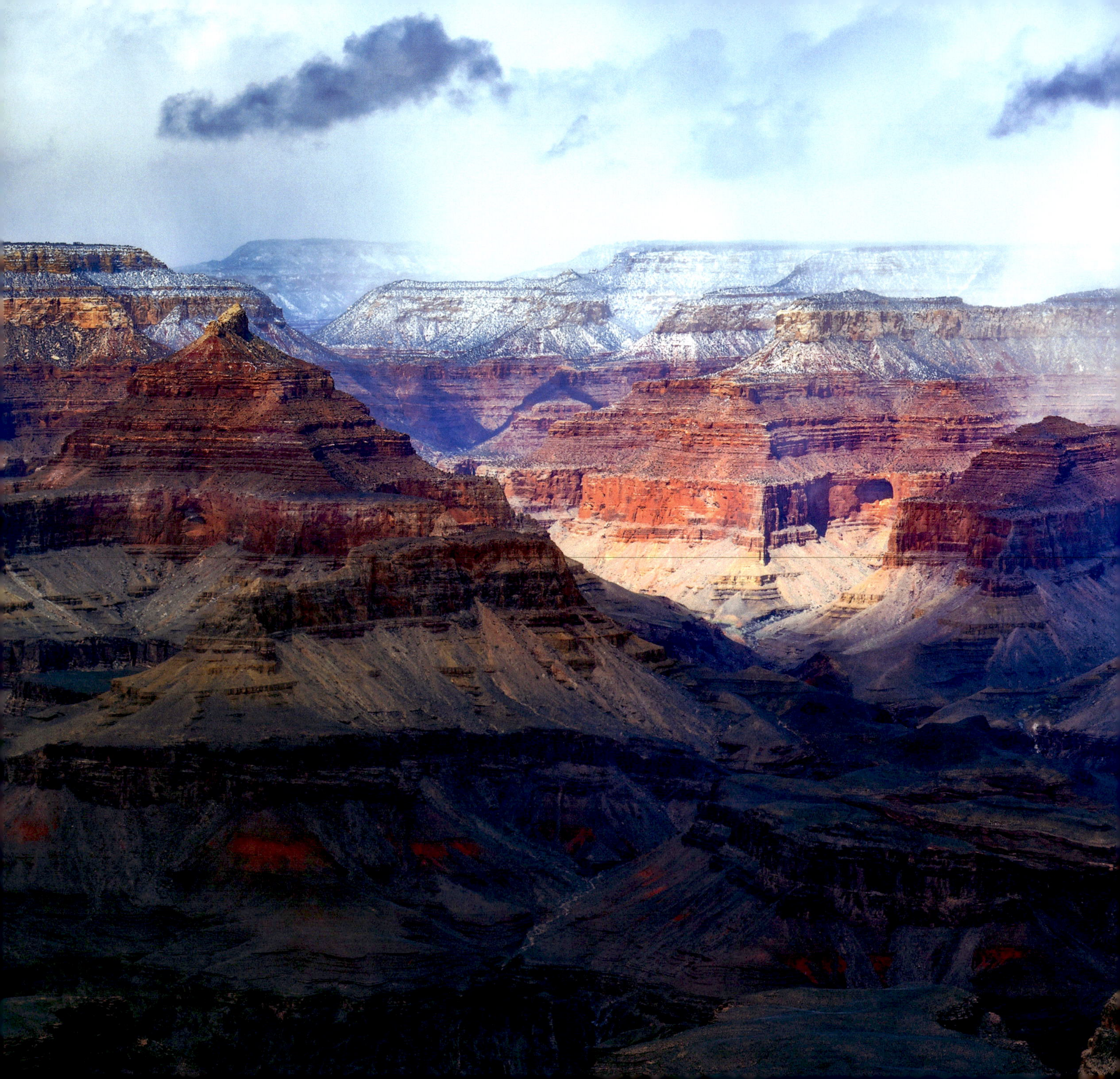

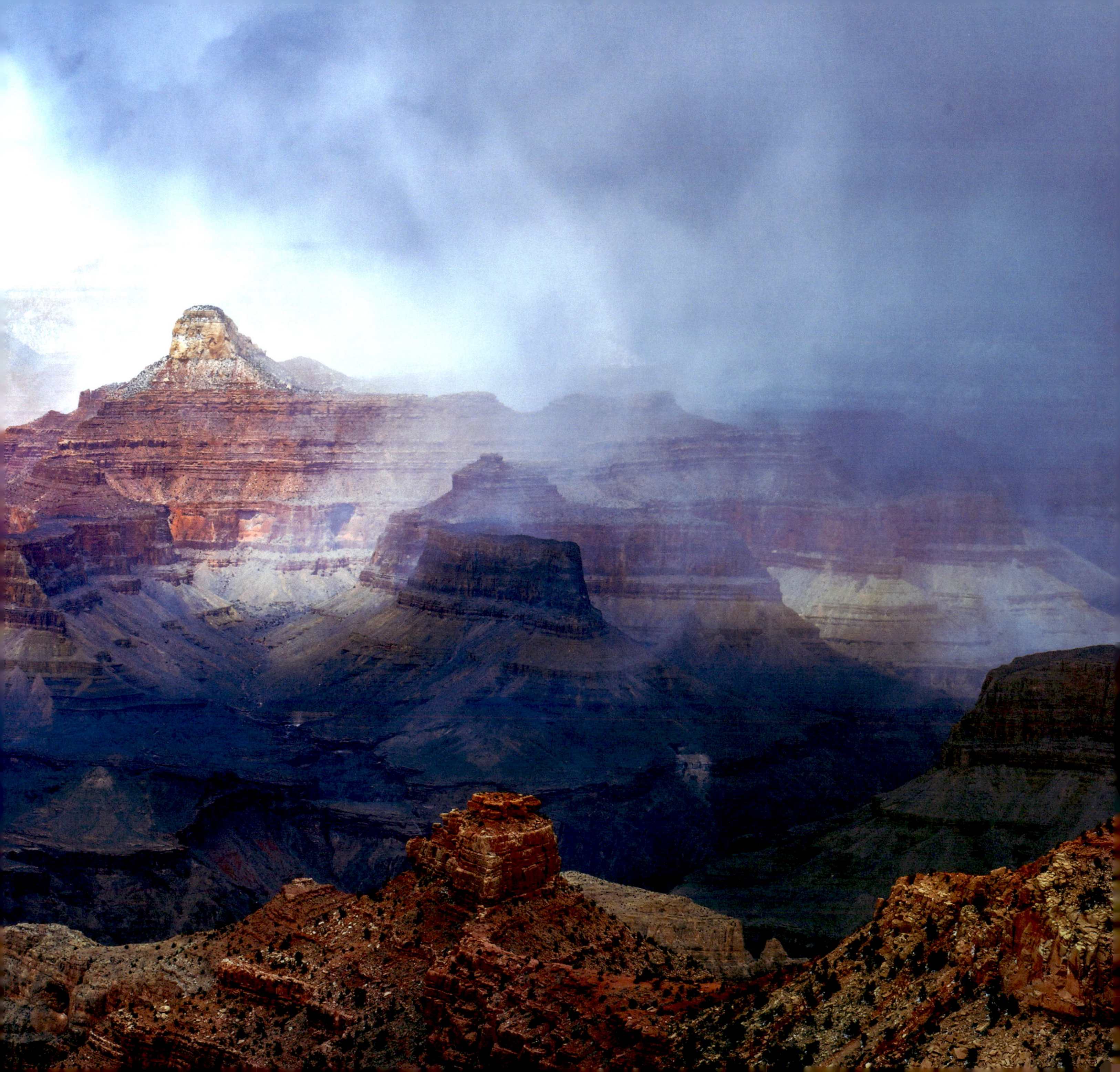

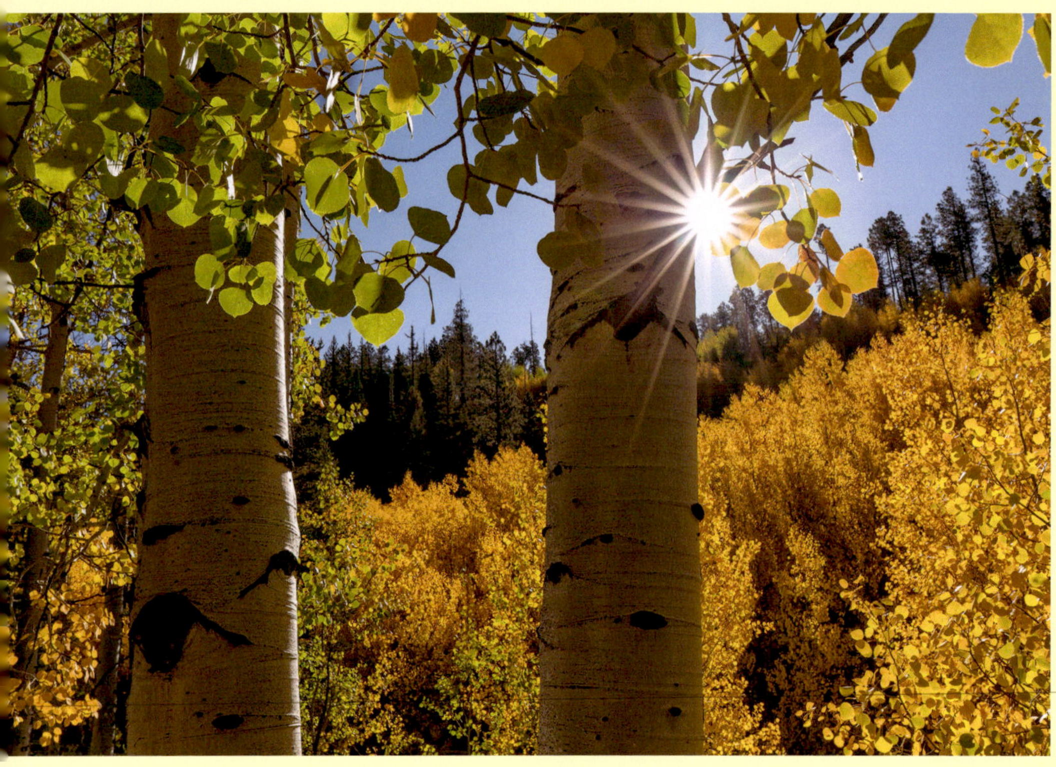

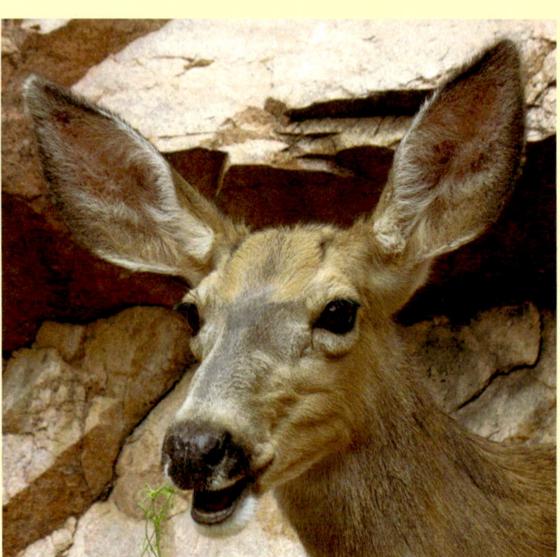

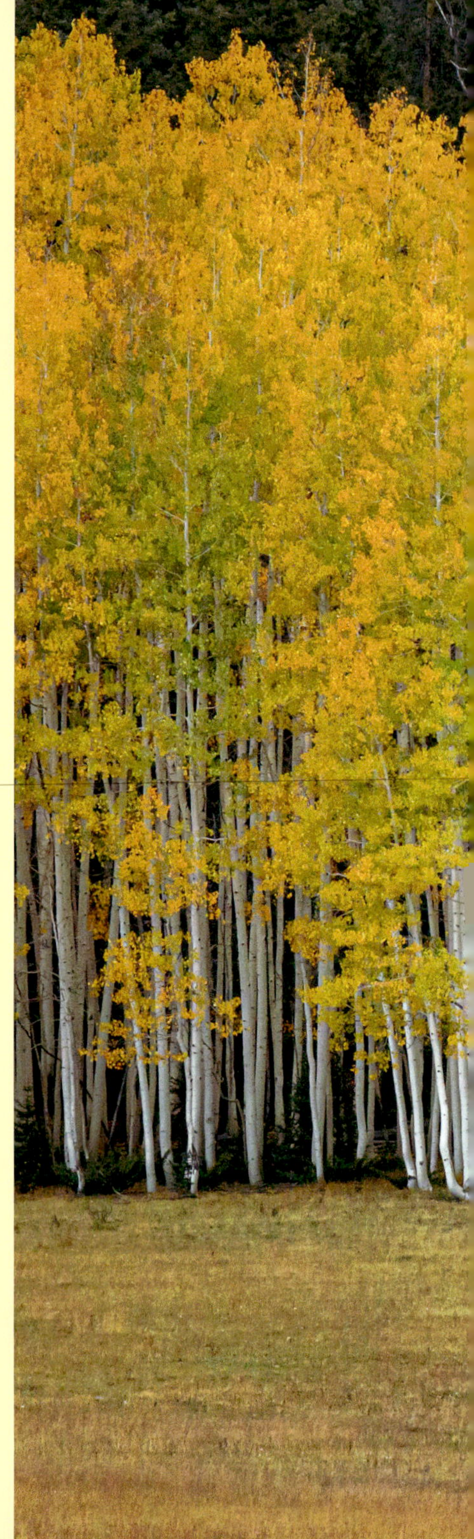

Above: Quaking aspen thrive in the higher, cooler conditions of the North Rim. Groves of aspen often grow as clones–interrelated trees all rising from a shared root system.

Right: The mule deer's large ears earned the species its common name, but they're also highly effective at detecting stealthy mountain lions, and at radiating excess body heat.

Far right: Edge habitat, such as where meadow meets forest, attracts wildlife, including the park's many mule deer.

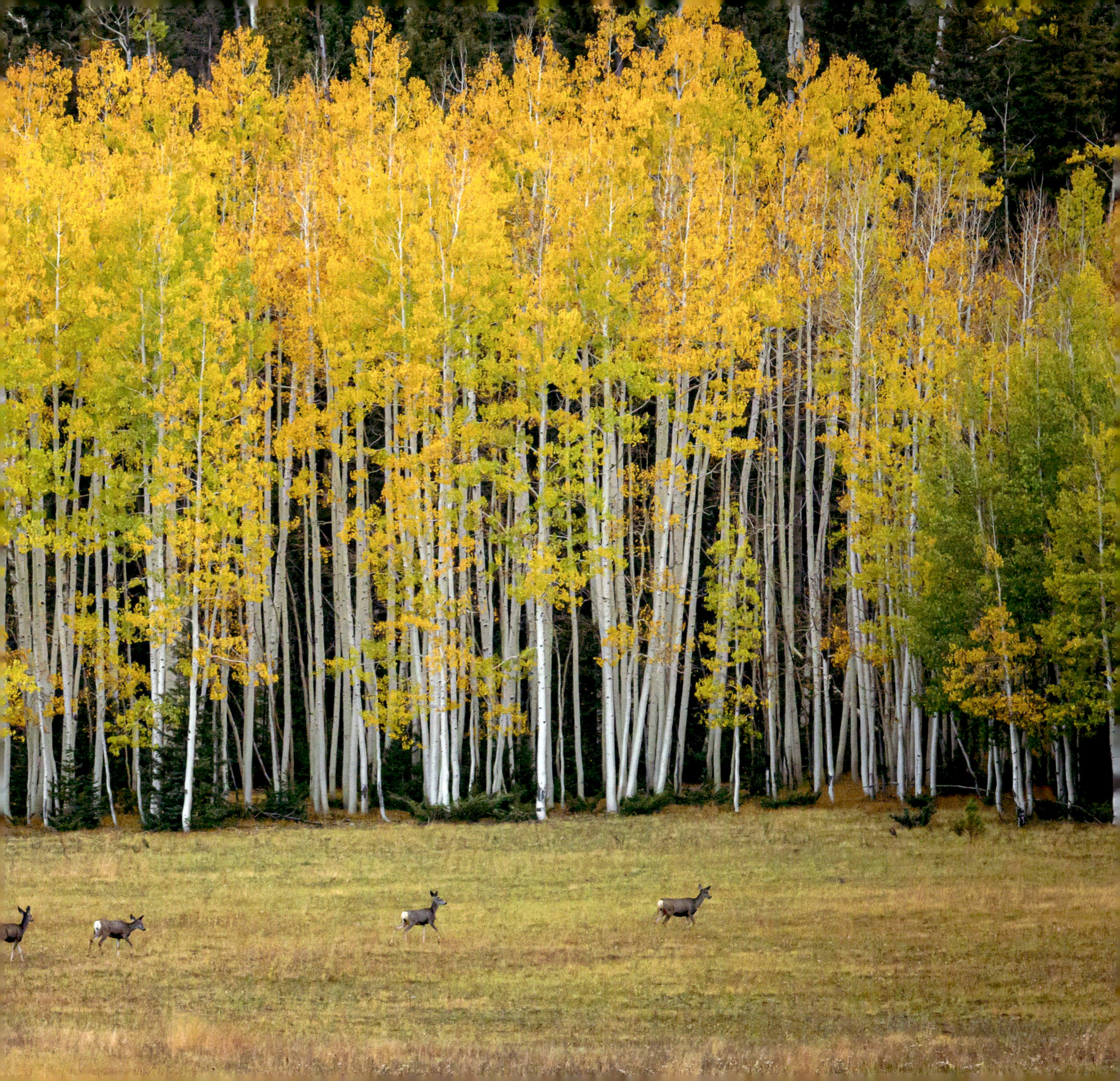

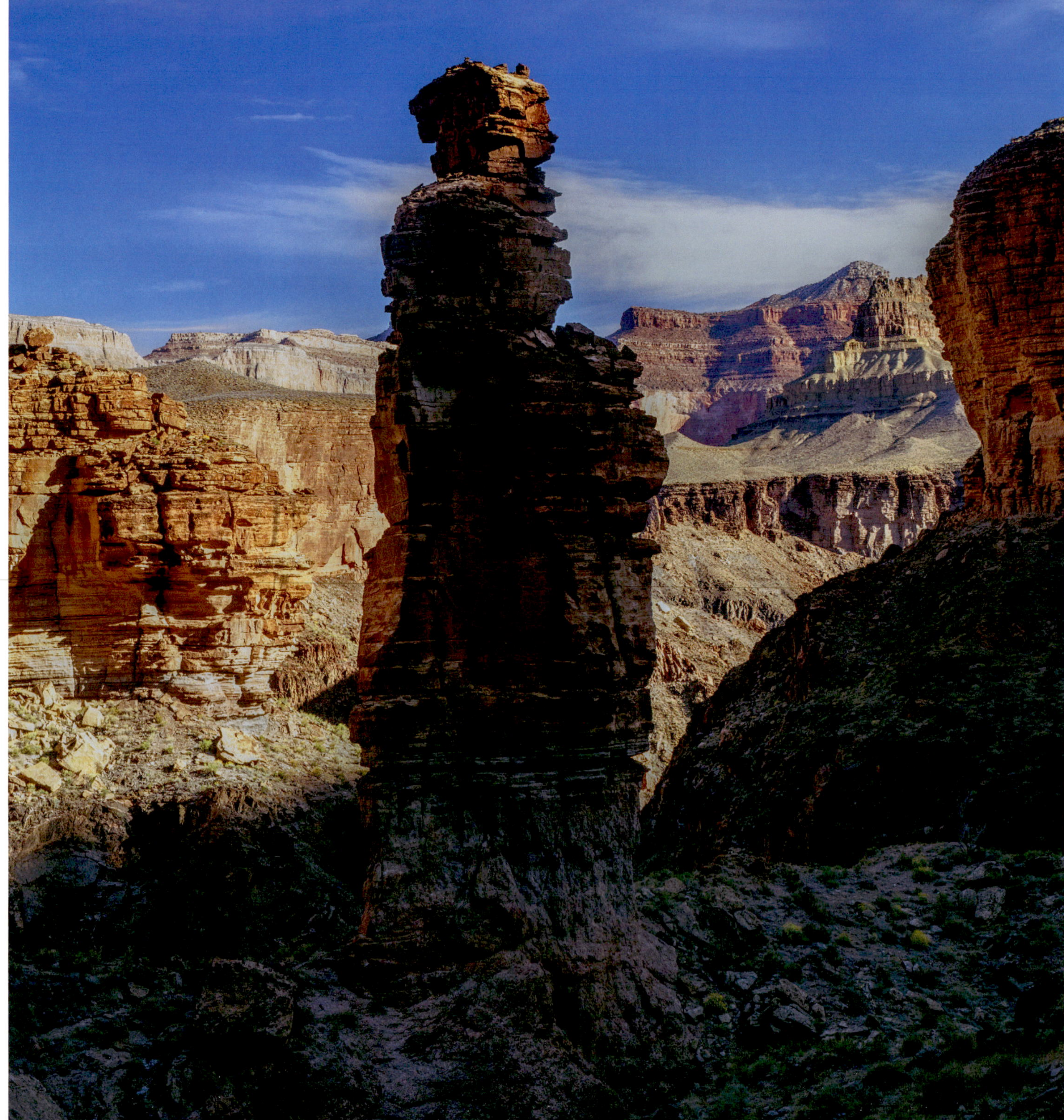

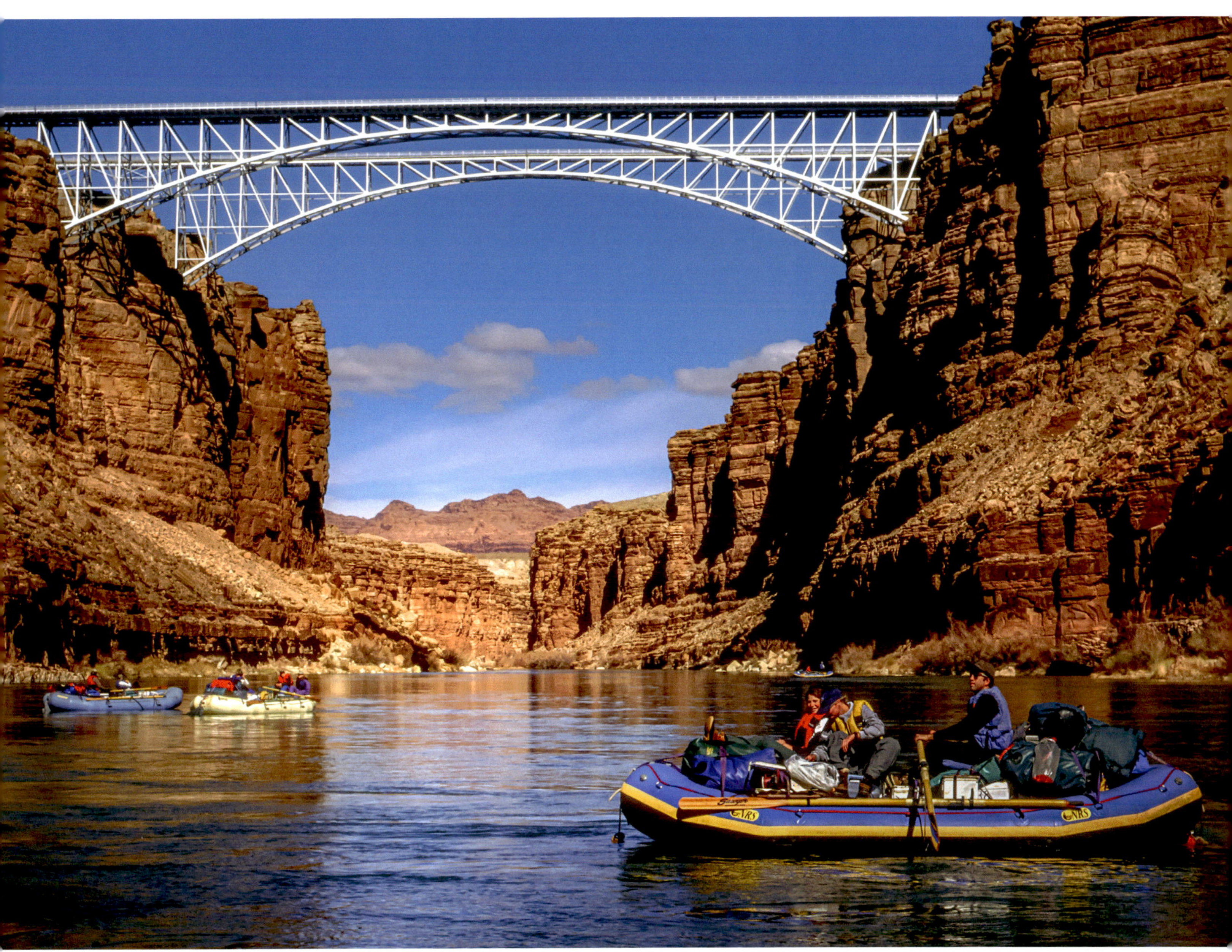

Above: Twin bridges span the Colorado River at the north end of the park. One carries U.S. Highway 89A, and its neighbor, the historic Navajo Bridge, now carries pedestrians. It's a popular spot to look for condors.

Facing page: This soaring pillar of Tapeats Sandstone and Zoroaster Granite gives Monument Creek Canyon its name.

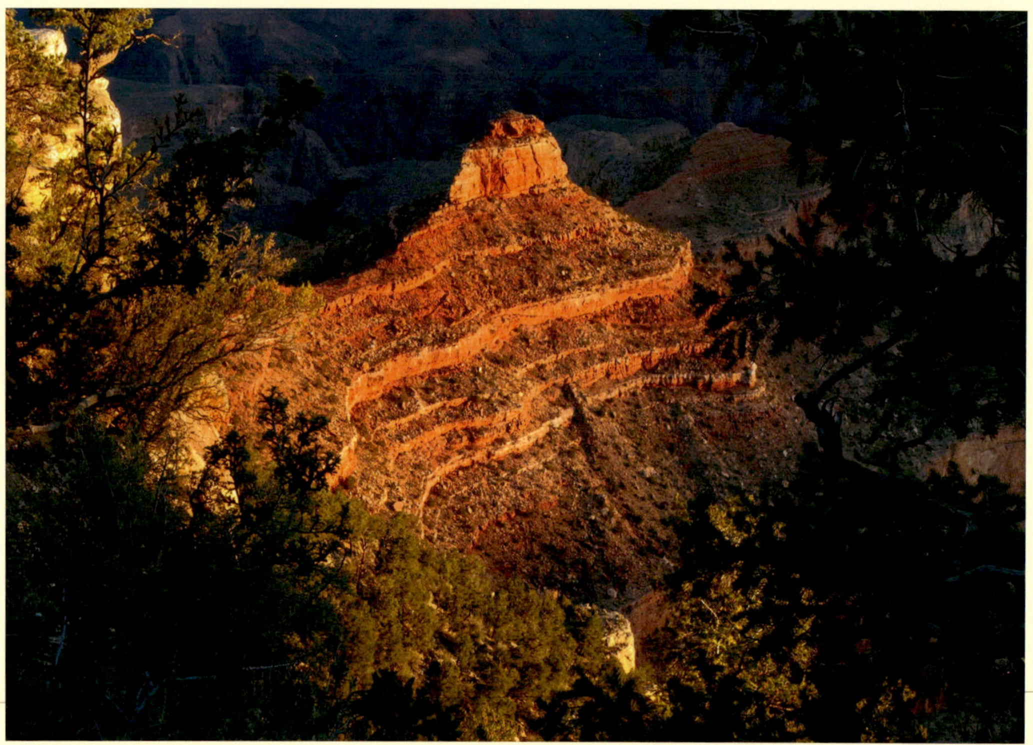

Above: Just north of Yaki Point, O'Neill Butte is named for William "Buckey" O'Neill, who prospected in the canyon and played a role in bringing the railroad to the South Rim. O'Neill later served with Teddy Roosevelt's Rough Riders and was killed in the Battle of San Juan Hill in Cuba.

Right: The cones of ponderosa pine shed seeds for two years. The seeds are a favorite food of Abert's squirrels and a wide variety of birds.

Far right: At 8,803 feet, Point Imperial is the highest point on the rim of the Grand Canyon. This sunlit spire rises just off the point.

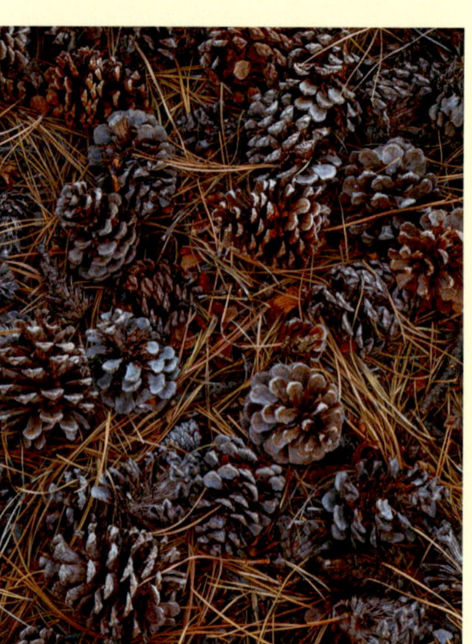

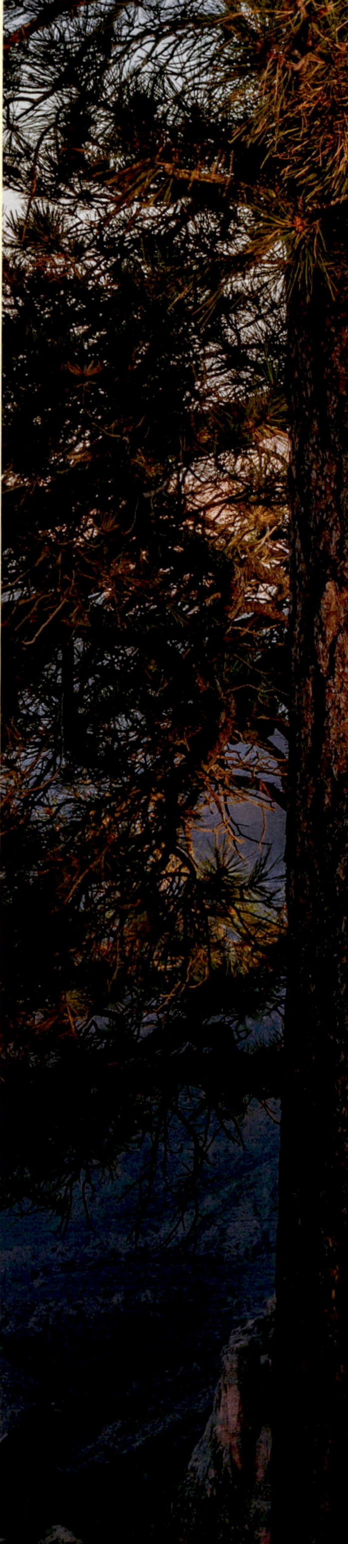

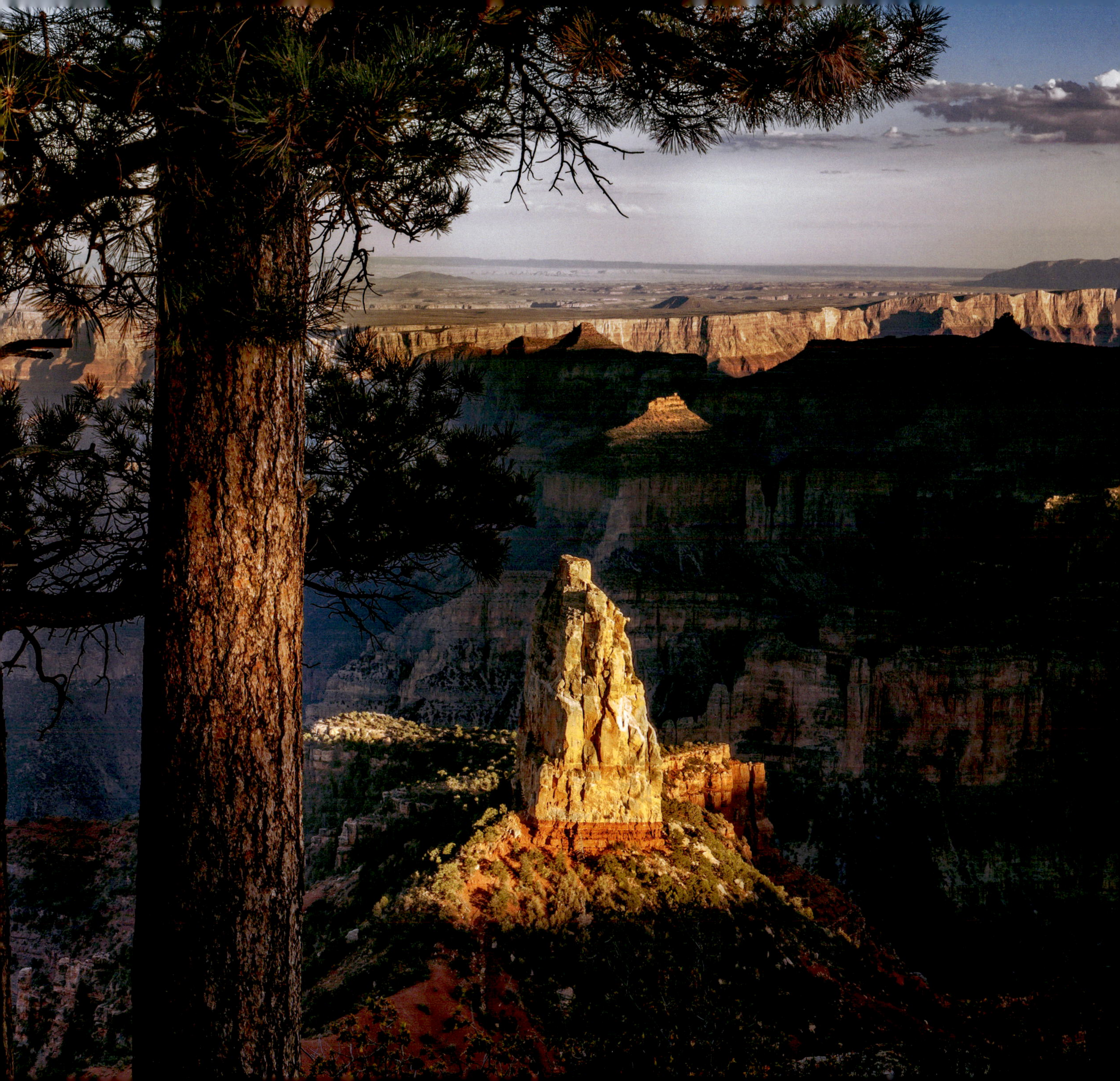

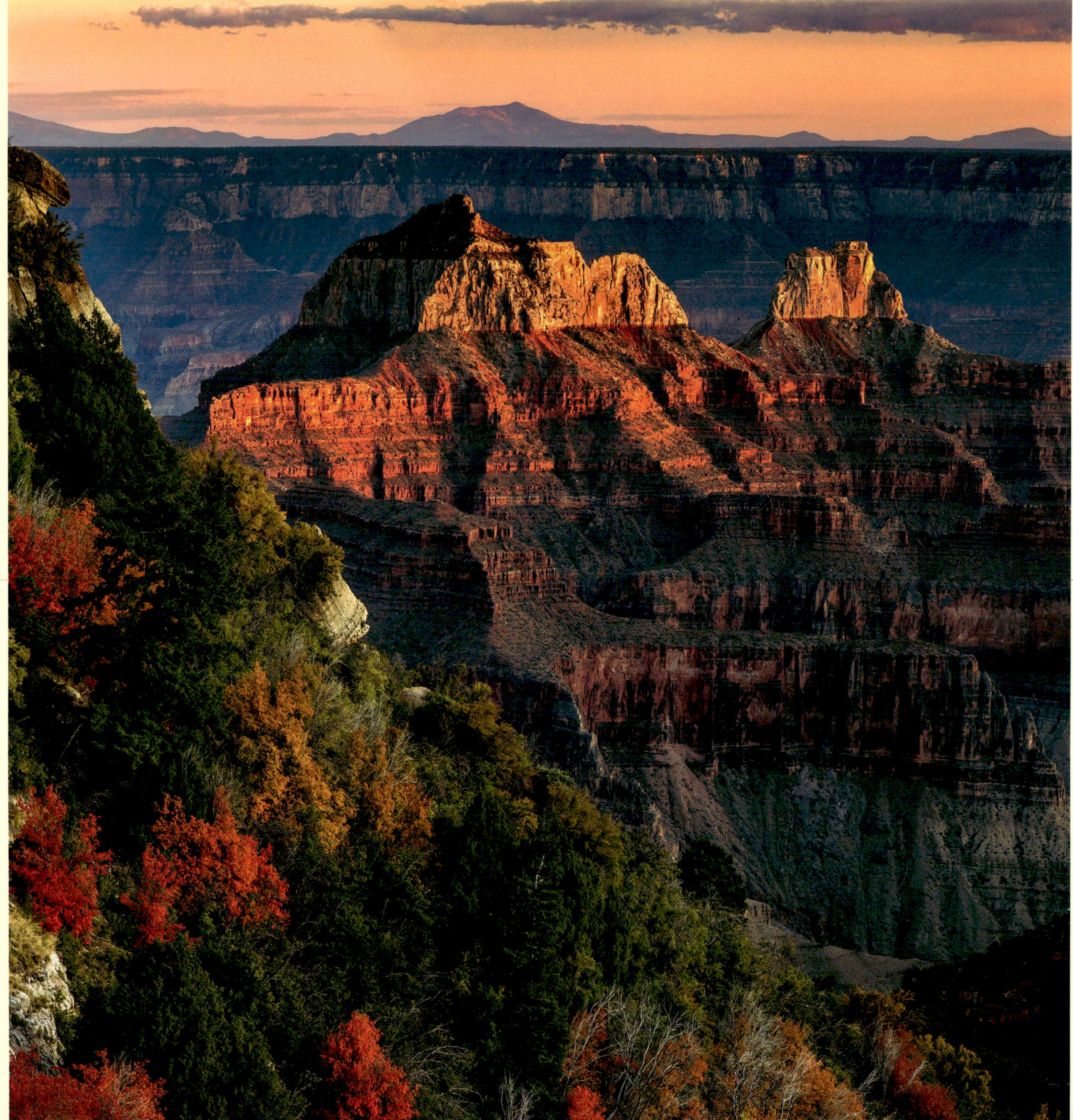

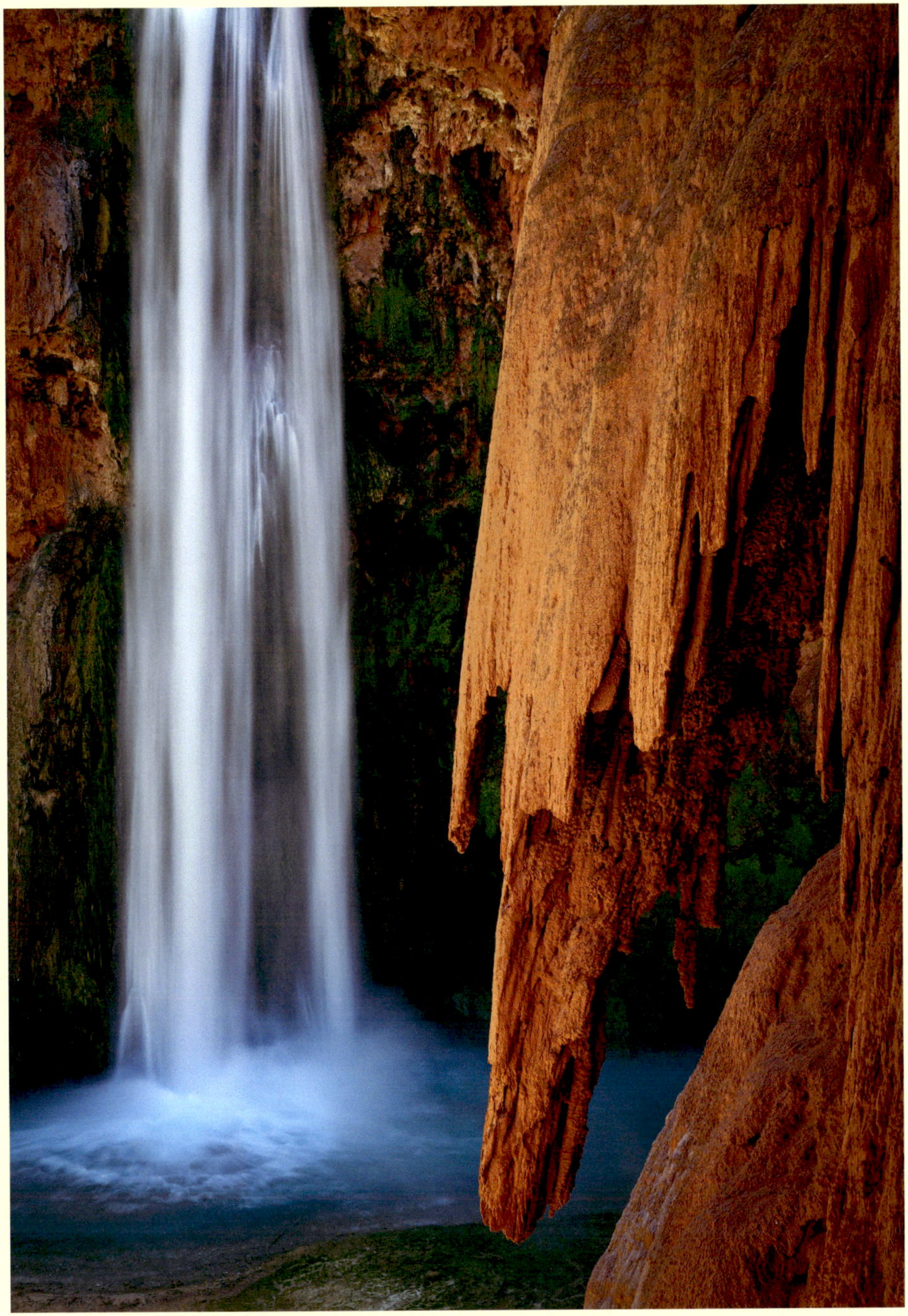

Left: Taller than Niagara Falls, Mooney Falls in Havasu Canyon plunges more than 200 feet down travertine cliffs into a turquoise pool.

Facing page: Fall foliage in Transept Canyon matches the sun-warmed cliffs of Brahma and Zoroaster Temples in the Grand Canyon.

Below: The Utah agave, also known as the century plant, blooms only once in its lifetime, sending a pulpy green stalk up to twenty feet above its basal leaves.

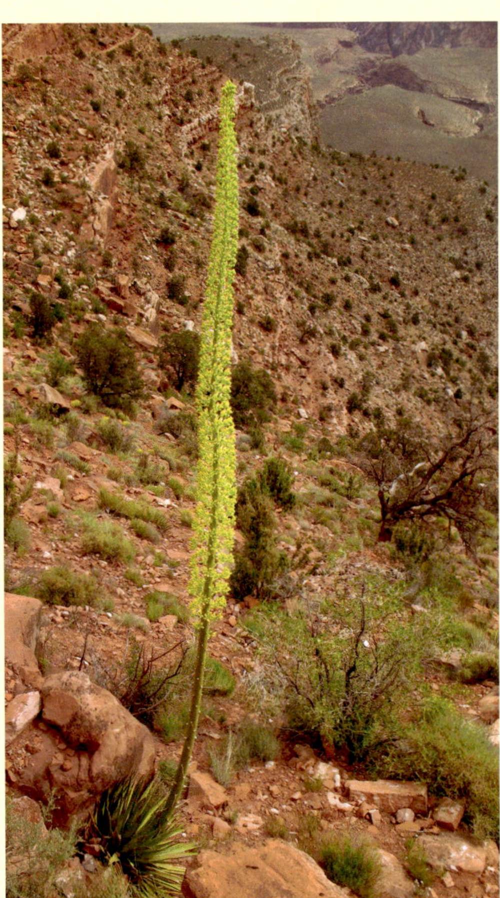

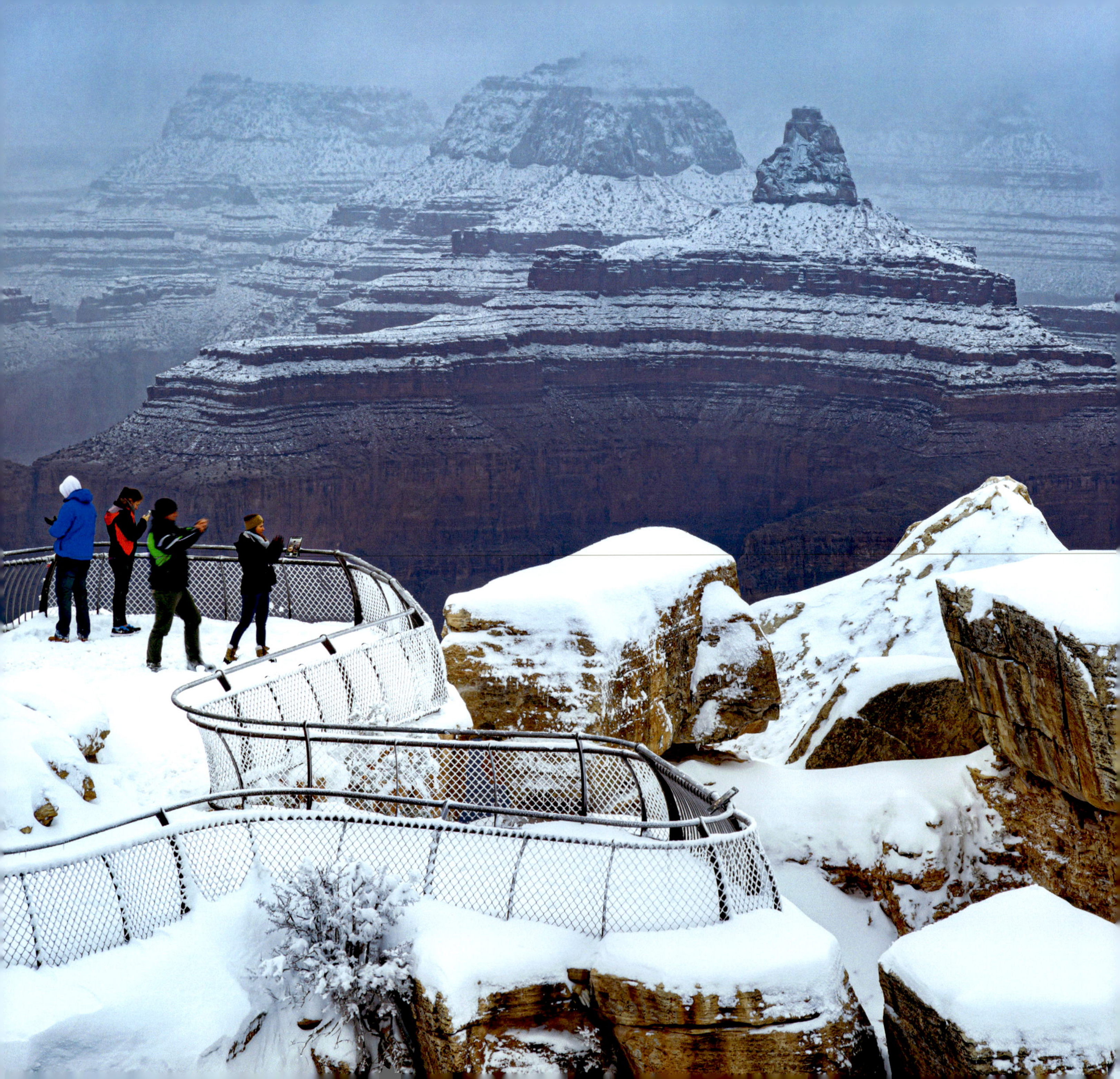

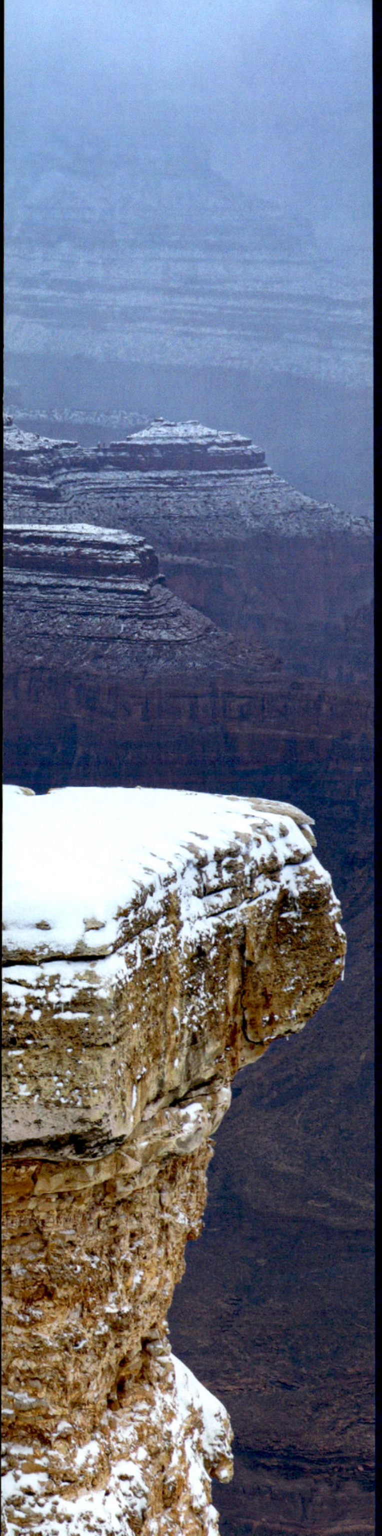

Right: Masters of canyon air currents, common ravens are also highly intelligent, naturally curious, and adept problem solvers.

Left: As seen from Mather Point on the South Rim, winter's mood in the canyon can be just as magical as any other season.

Below: Work at the park doesn't stop for snow. A wrangler leads pack mules down the Bright Angel Trail in February.

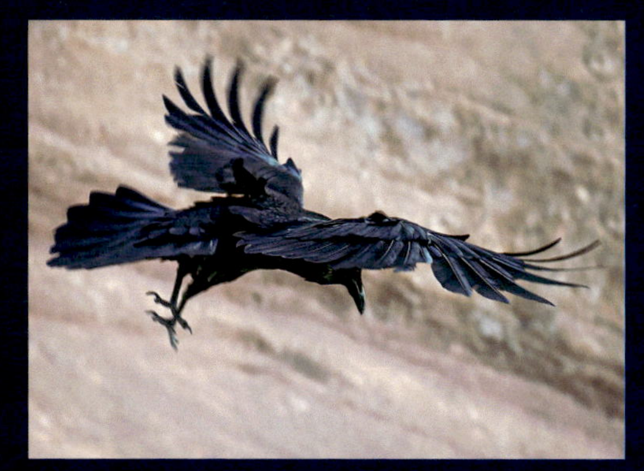

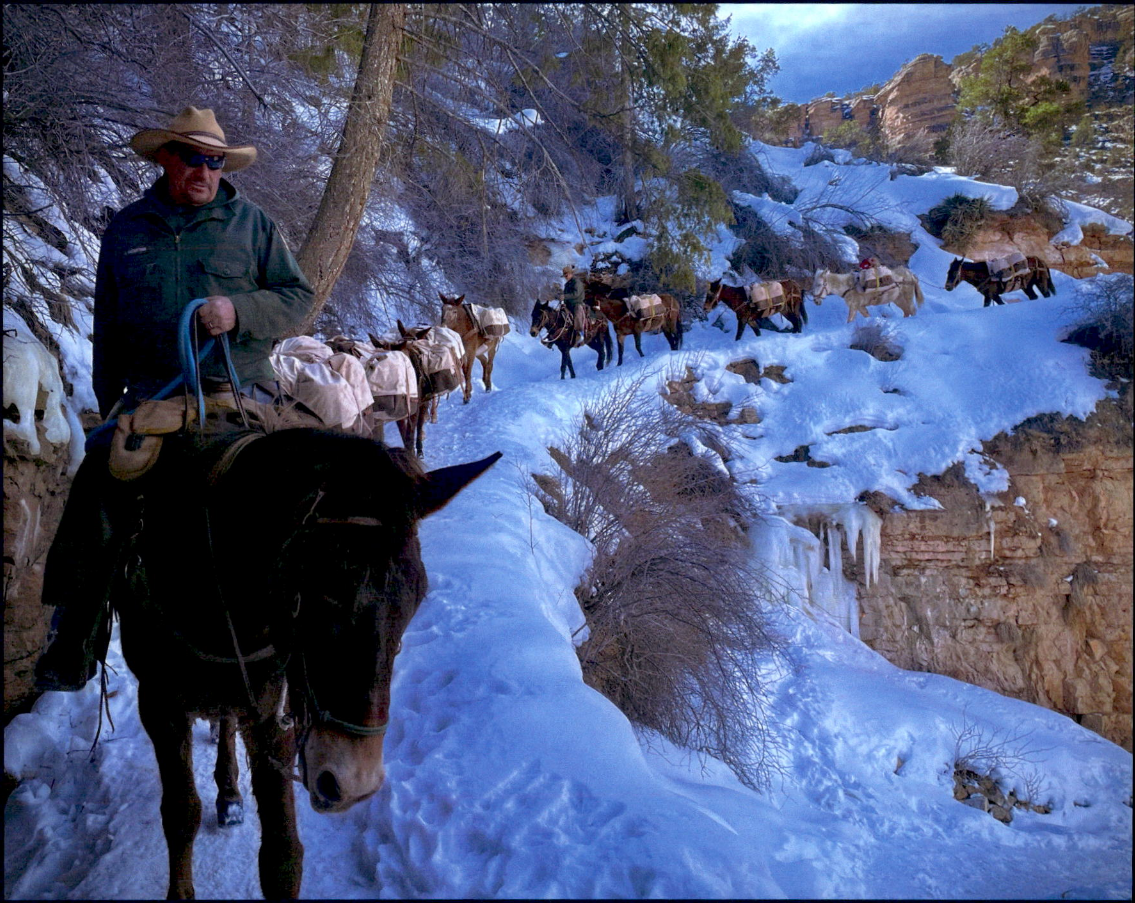

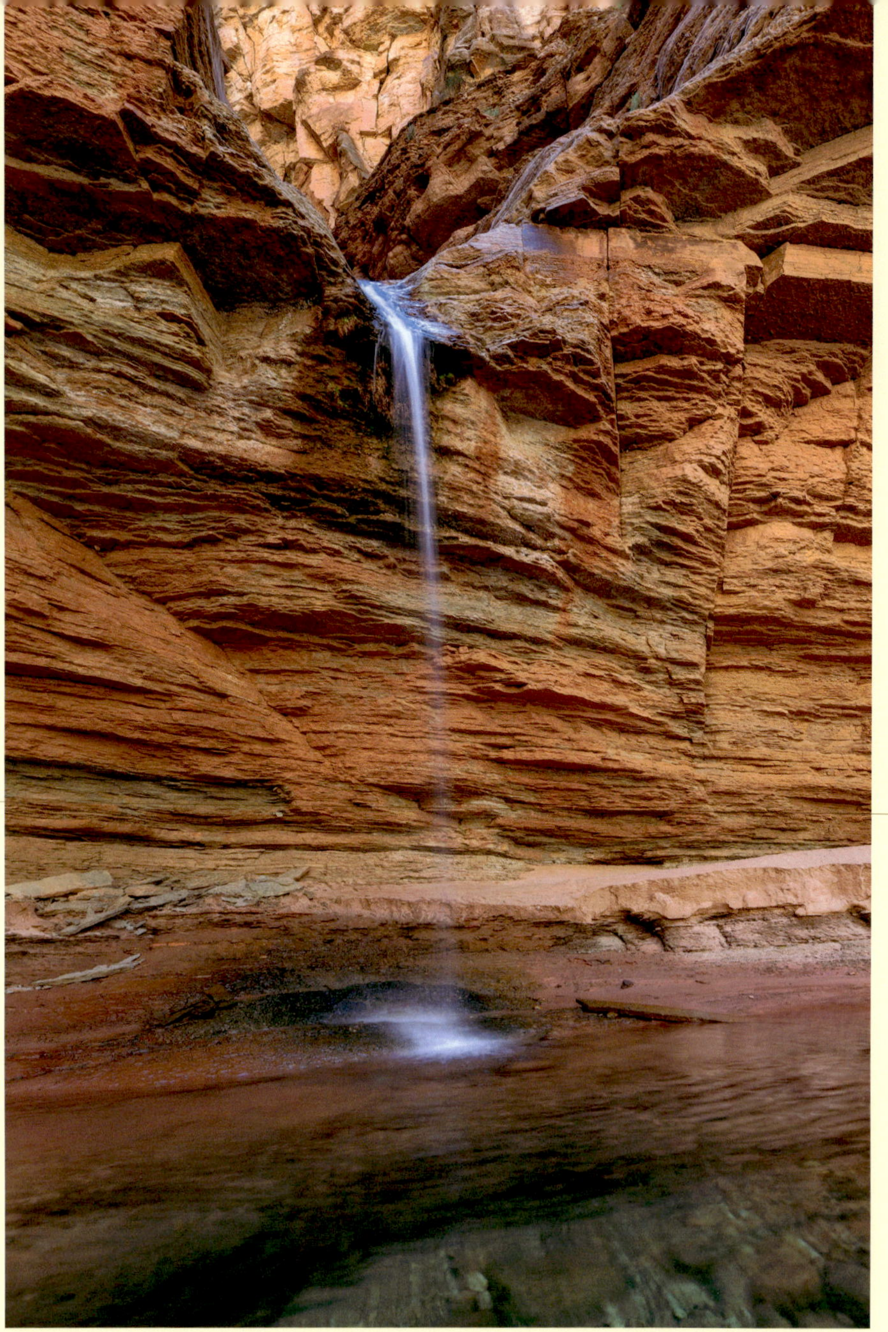

Above: A waterfall spills out of Olo Canyon at river mile 145.5.

Right: A new day brings new vistas to Navajo Point on the South Rim.

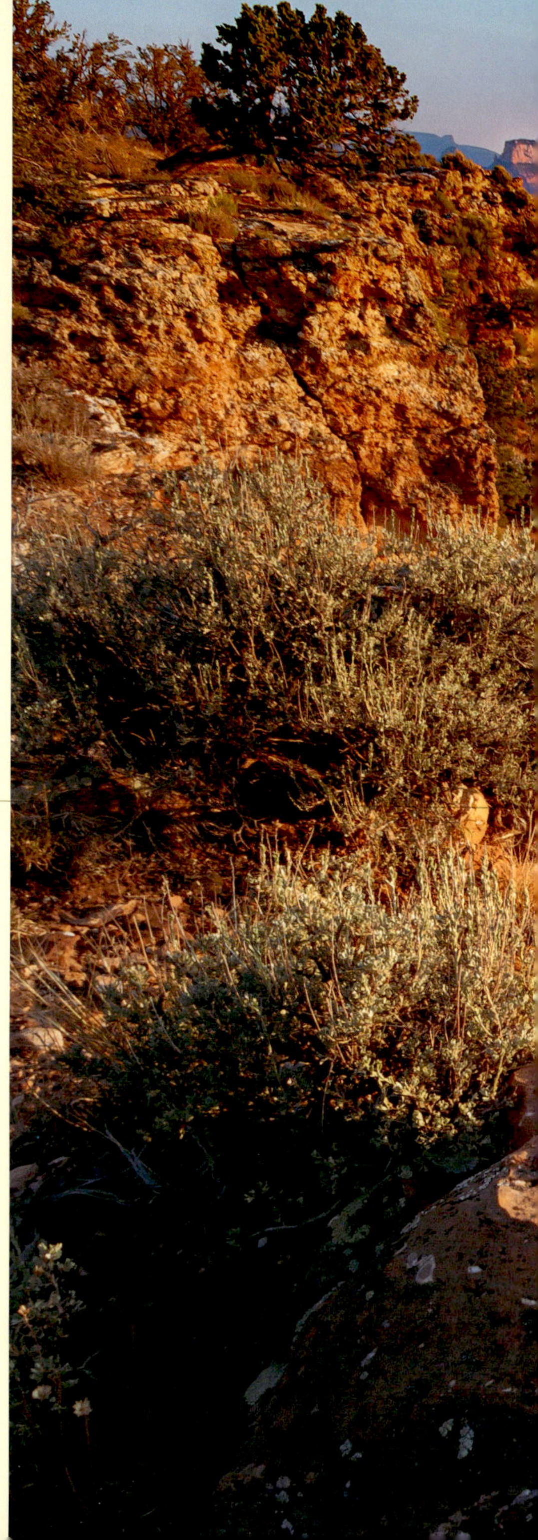

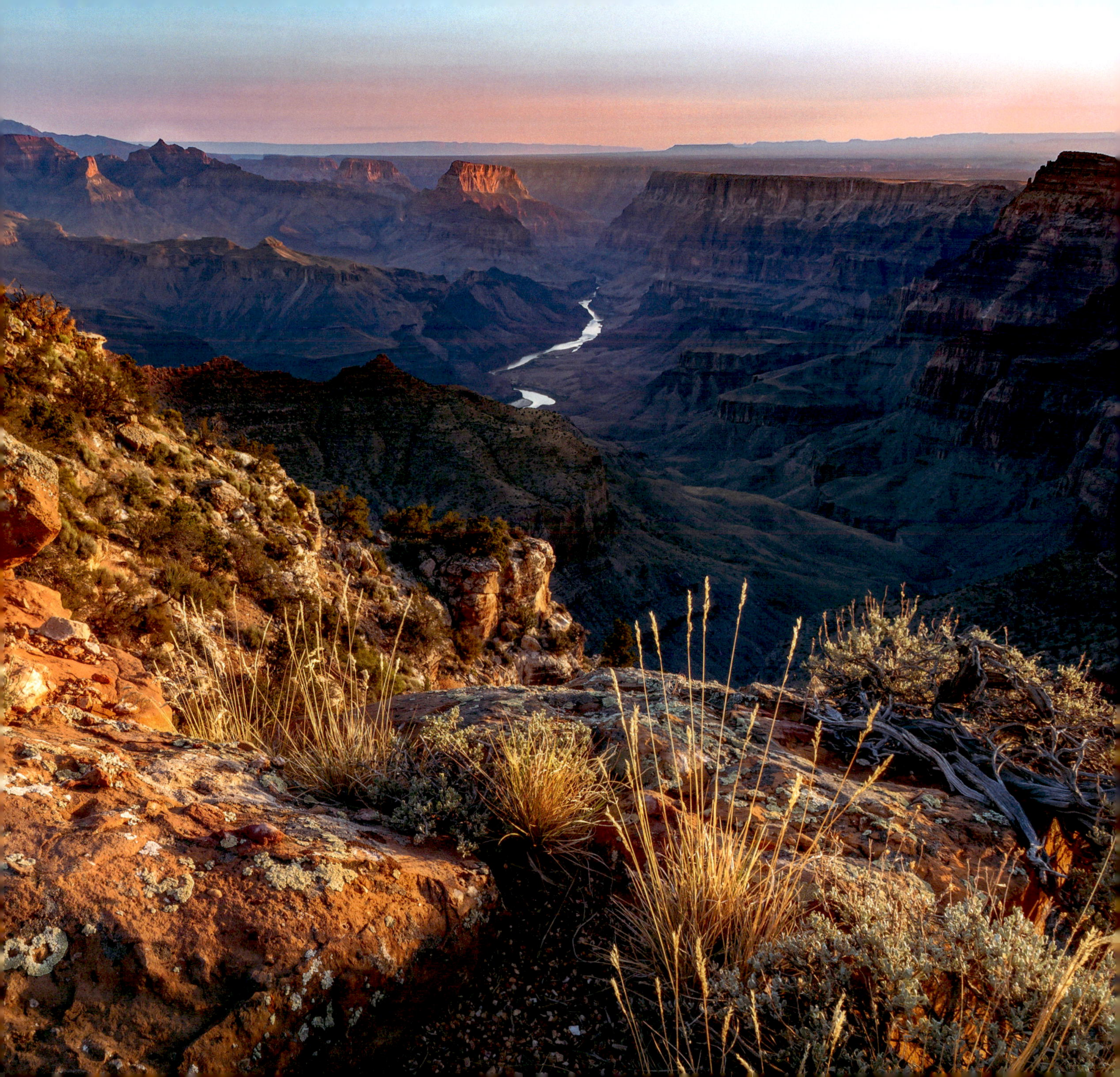

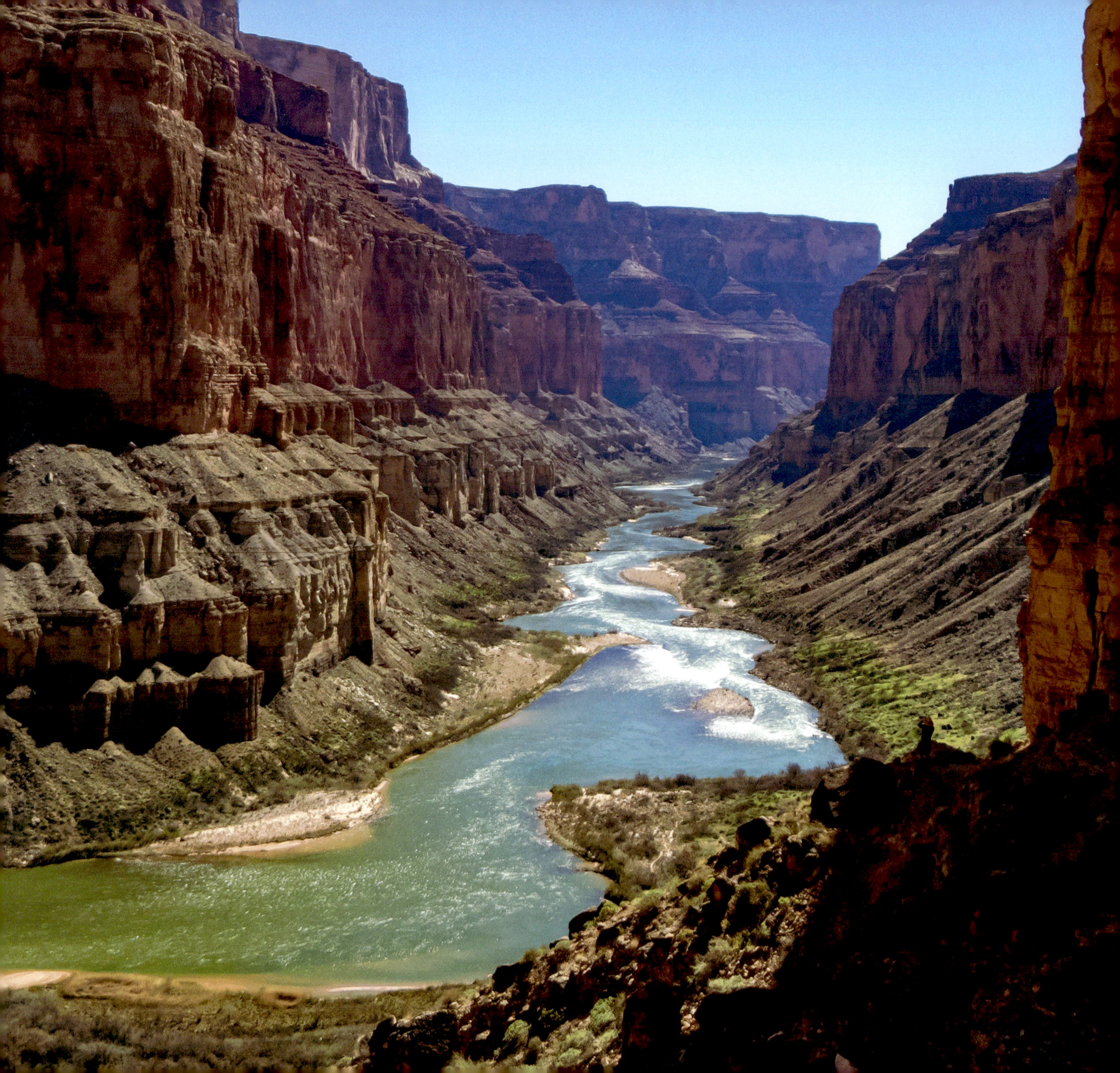

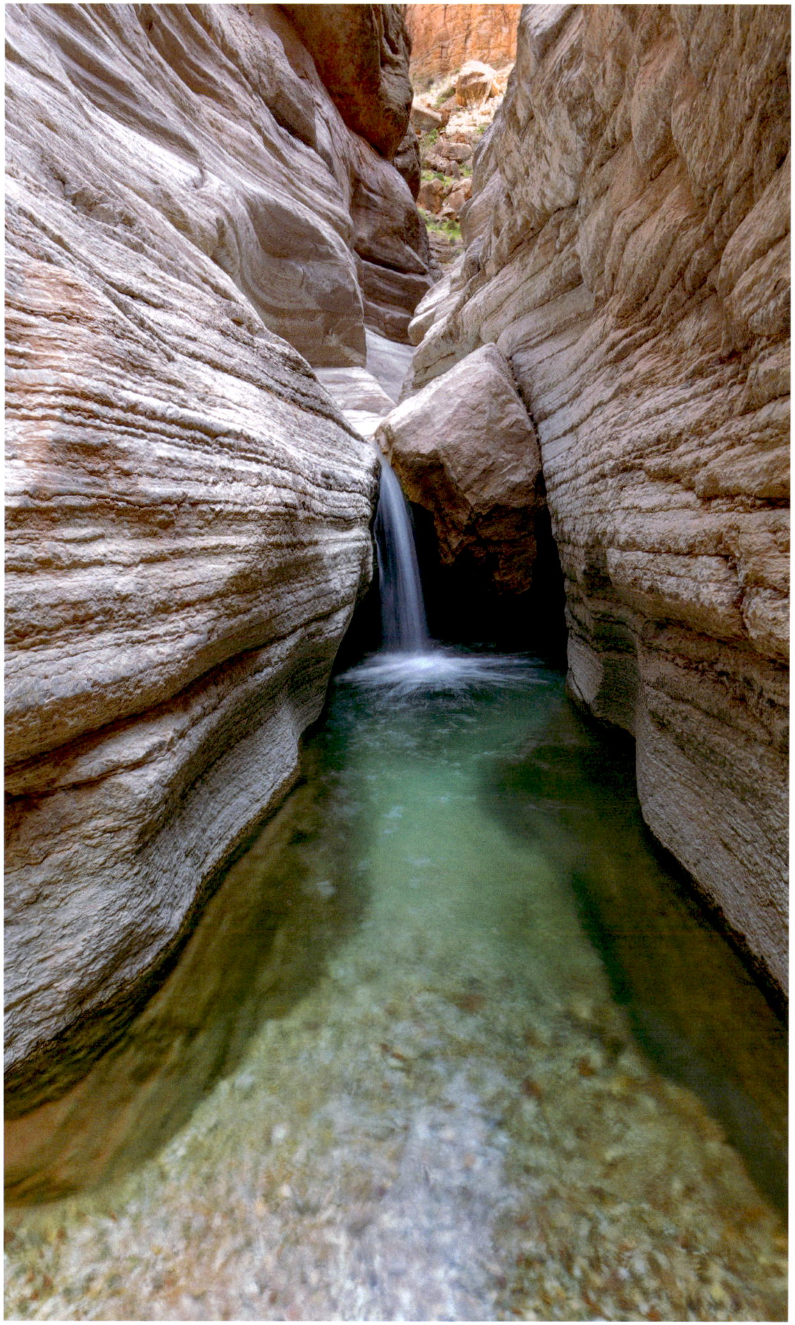

Left: A narrow side canyon at river mile 166 reveals the stone-carving power of water.

Far left: Floating the Colorado River affords countless opportunities for day hikes and scenic views.

Below: Rich in fossils, Grand Canyon's rocks hold evidence of life dating back 1.2 billion years. The nautiloid fossil here likely dates to nearly 300 million years ago. Visitors are welcome to photograph their fossil finds, but please leave them undisturbed.

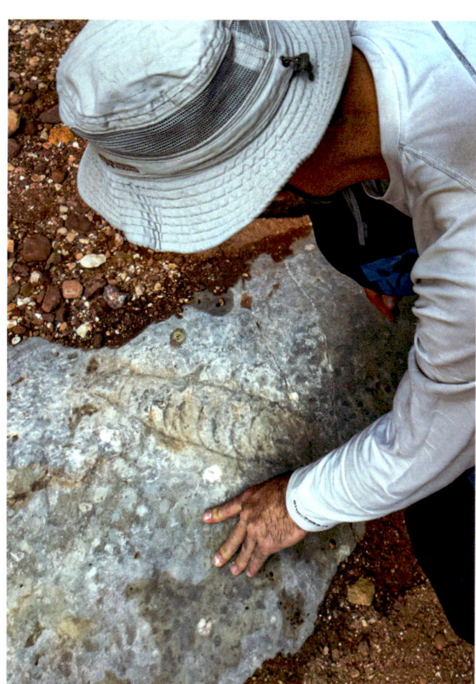

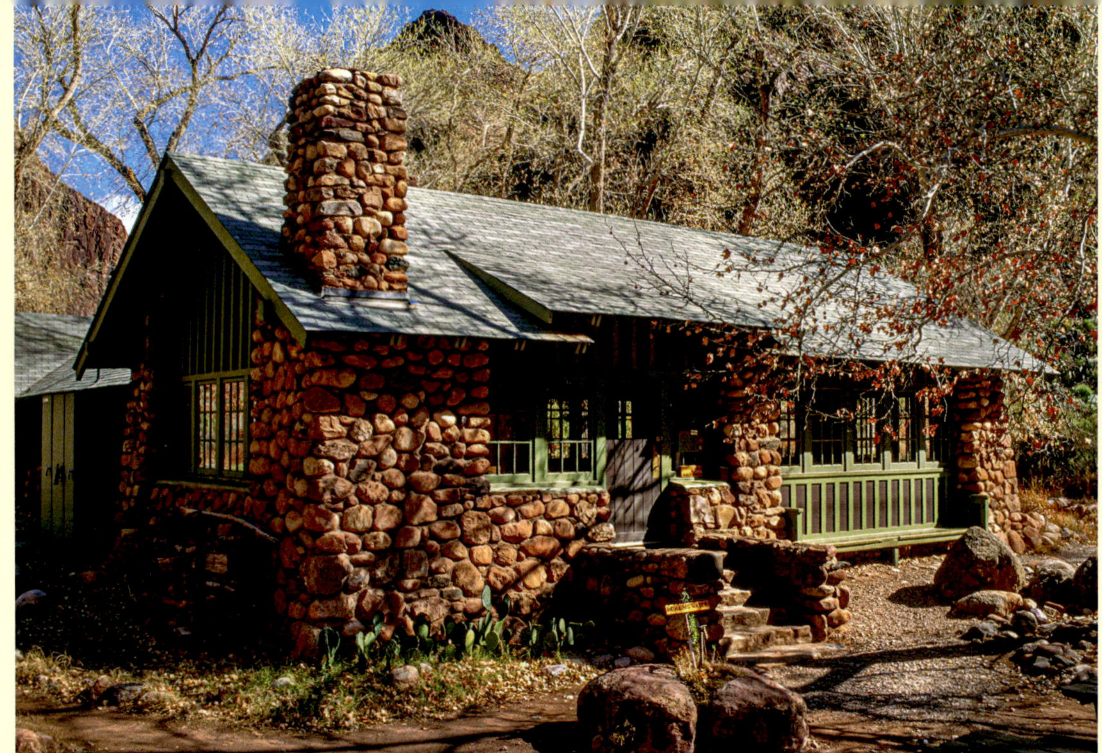

Right: Hikers and mule riders alike find respite at Phantom Ranch in the bottom of the Grand Canyon. The Mary Colter-designed canteen serves sit-down breakfast and dinner; sack lunches are also available.

Facing page: About 1,000 years ago, an extended Ancestral Puebloan family lived at the Bright Angel Site at the mouth of Bright Angel Creek near Phantom Ranch. Today, interpretive panels describe daily life in this oasis at the canyon's bottom.

Below: Architect Mary Colter used wood and native stone to ensure the cabins at Phantom Ranch would blend with their surroundings.

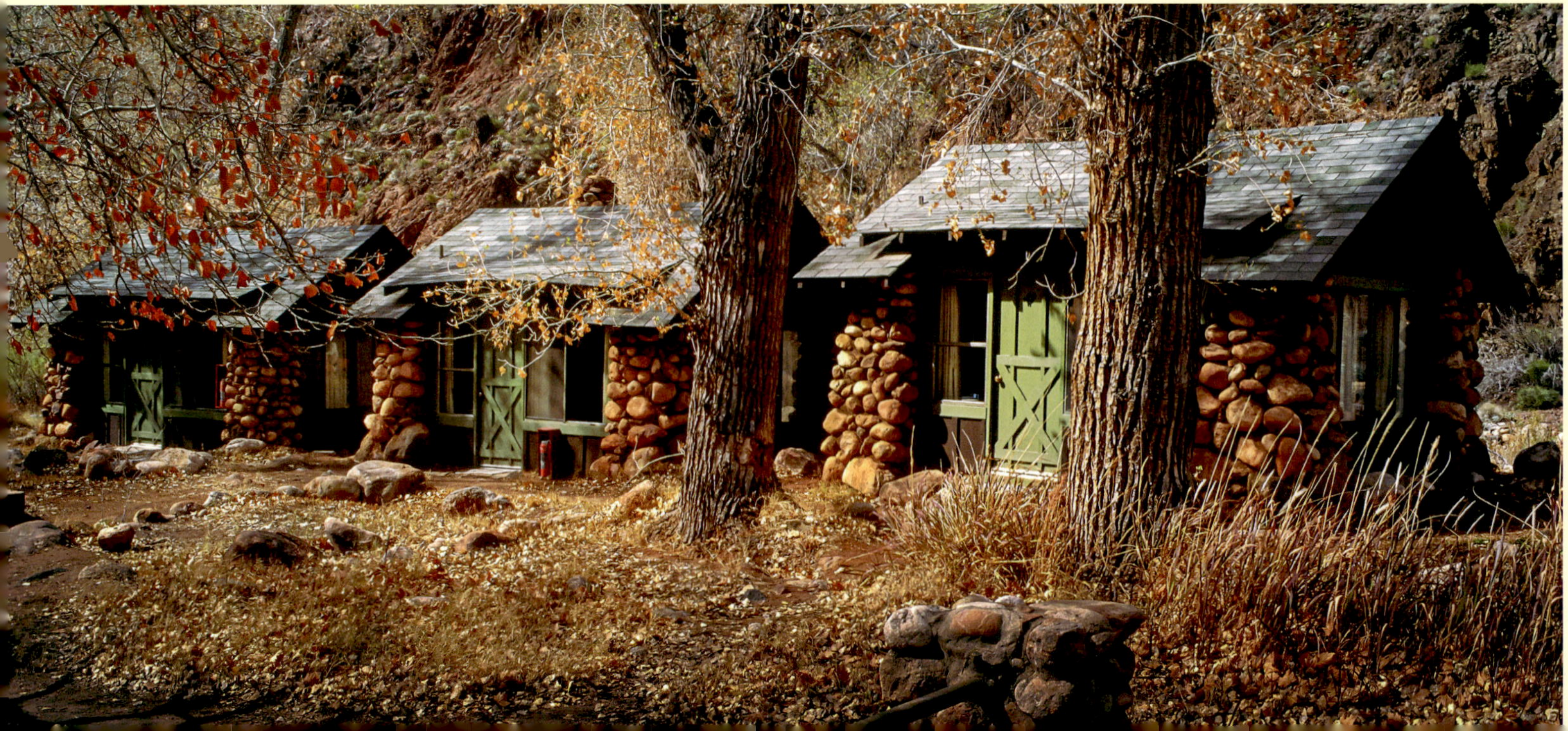

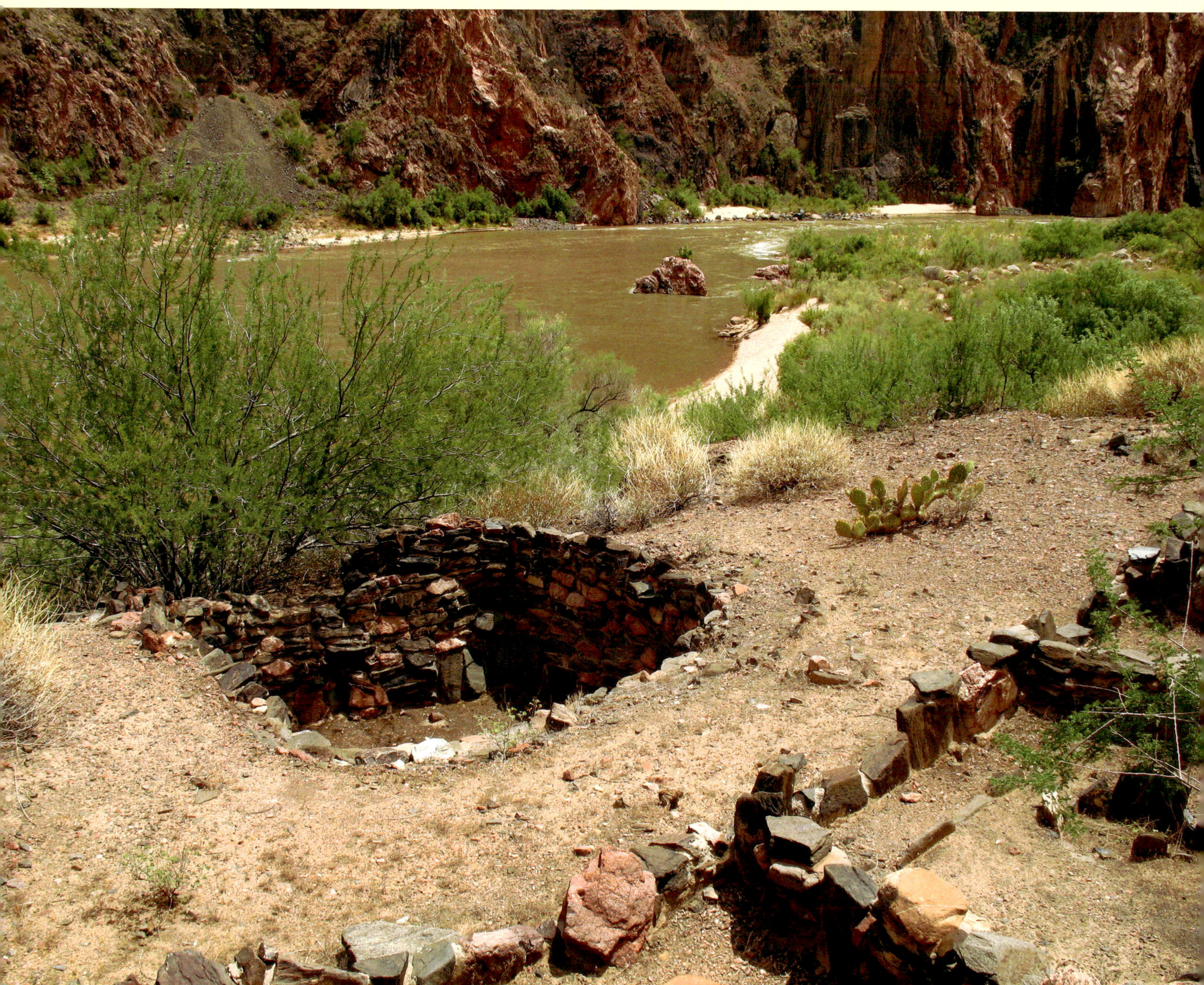

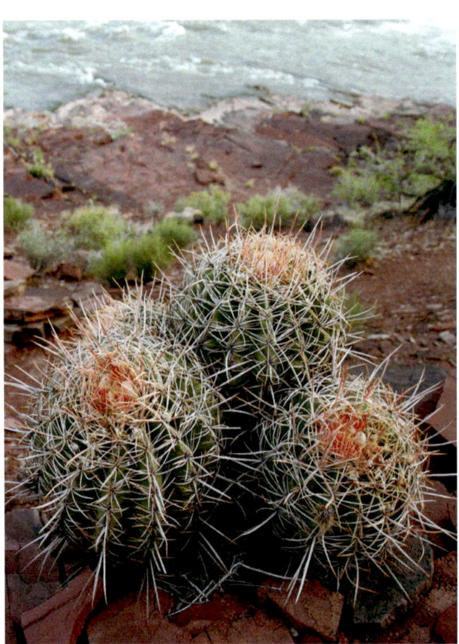

Right: More than two dozen species of cactus are found within the park, most in the inner canyon.

Far right: Rafters enjoy a stretch of placid water on the Colorado River near Point Hansbrough.

Below: In 1915, three men attempted to run the Colorado River in this metal rowboat, built by Bert Loper and named the *Ross Wheeler* in honor of a local steamboat pilot. They were hoping to make a motion picture of their feat, but the boat proved unwieldly and they abandoned it at Bass Rapids, climbing out of the canyon. The park service chained the *Ross Wheeler* in place in 1984.

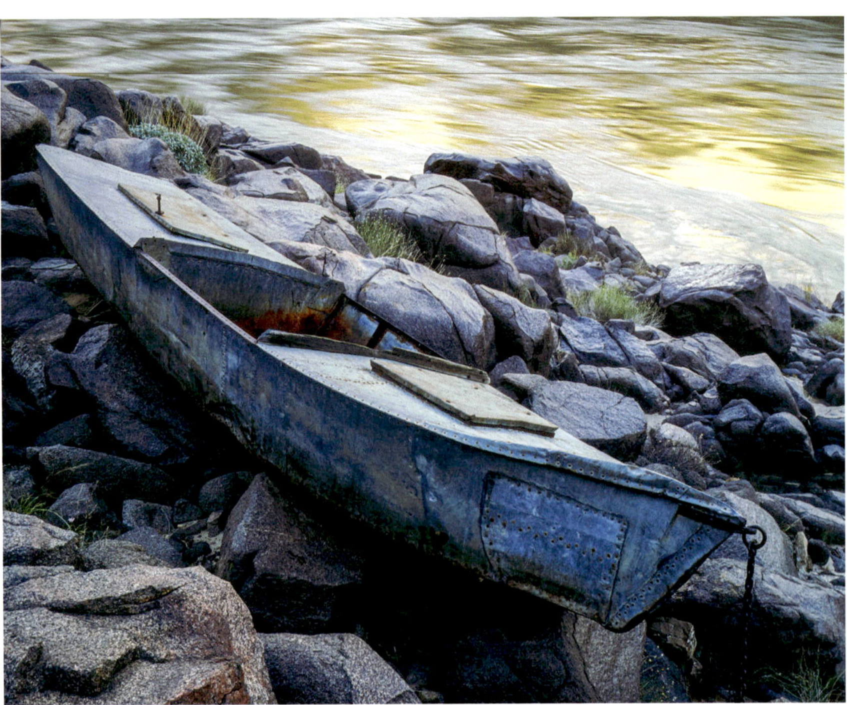

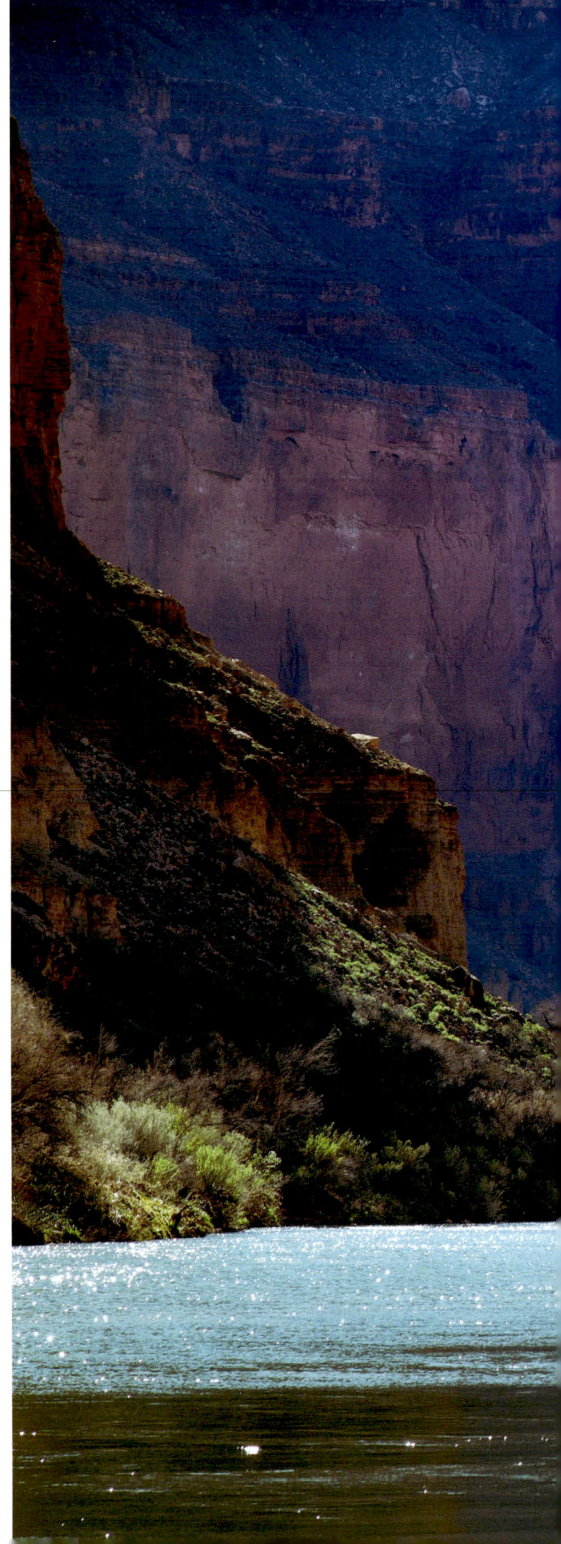

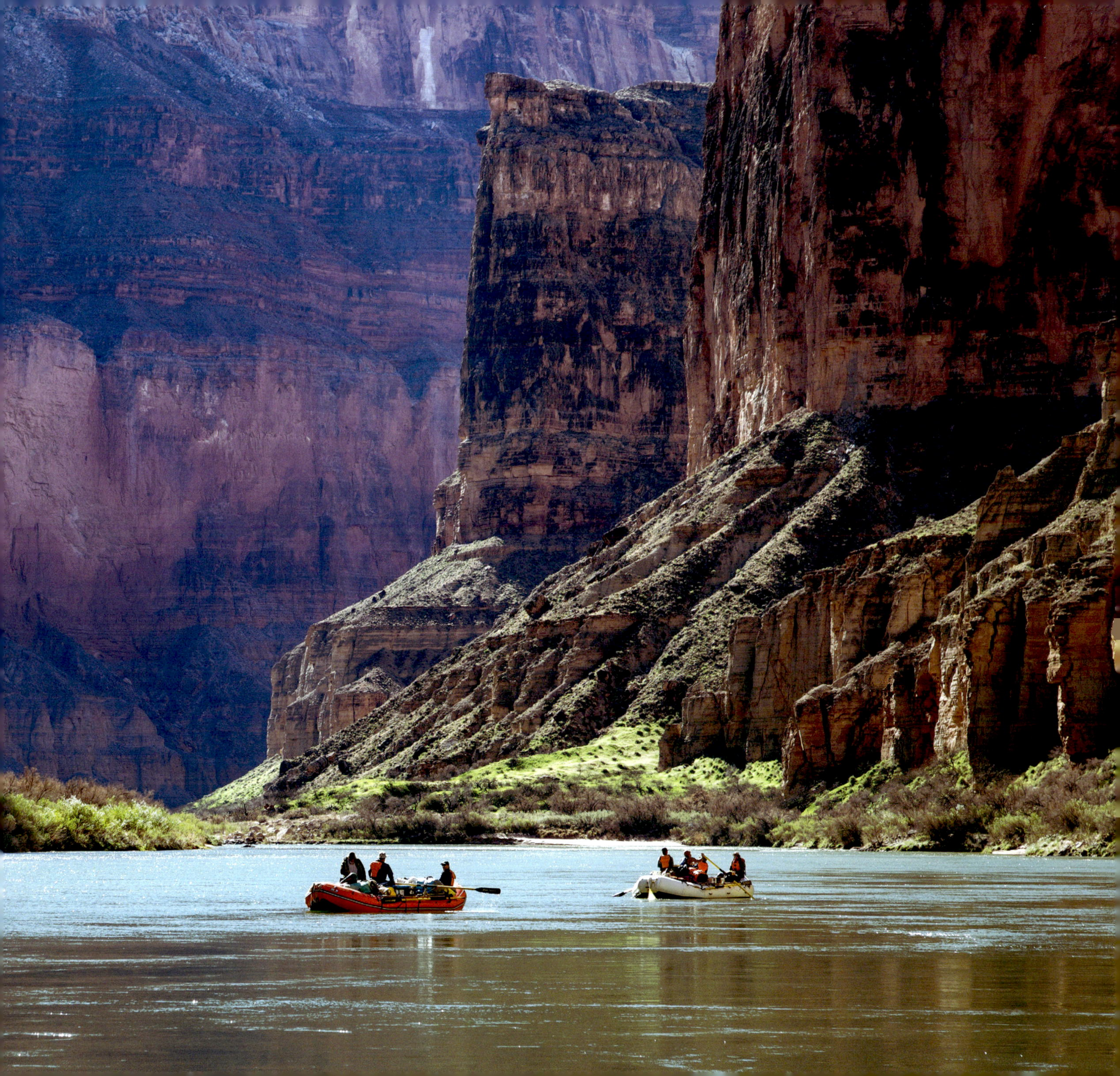

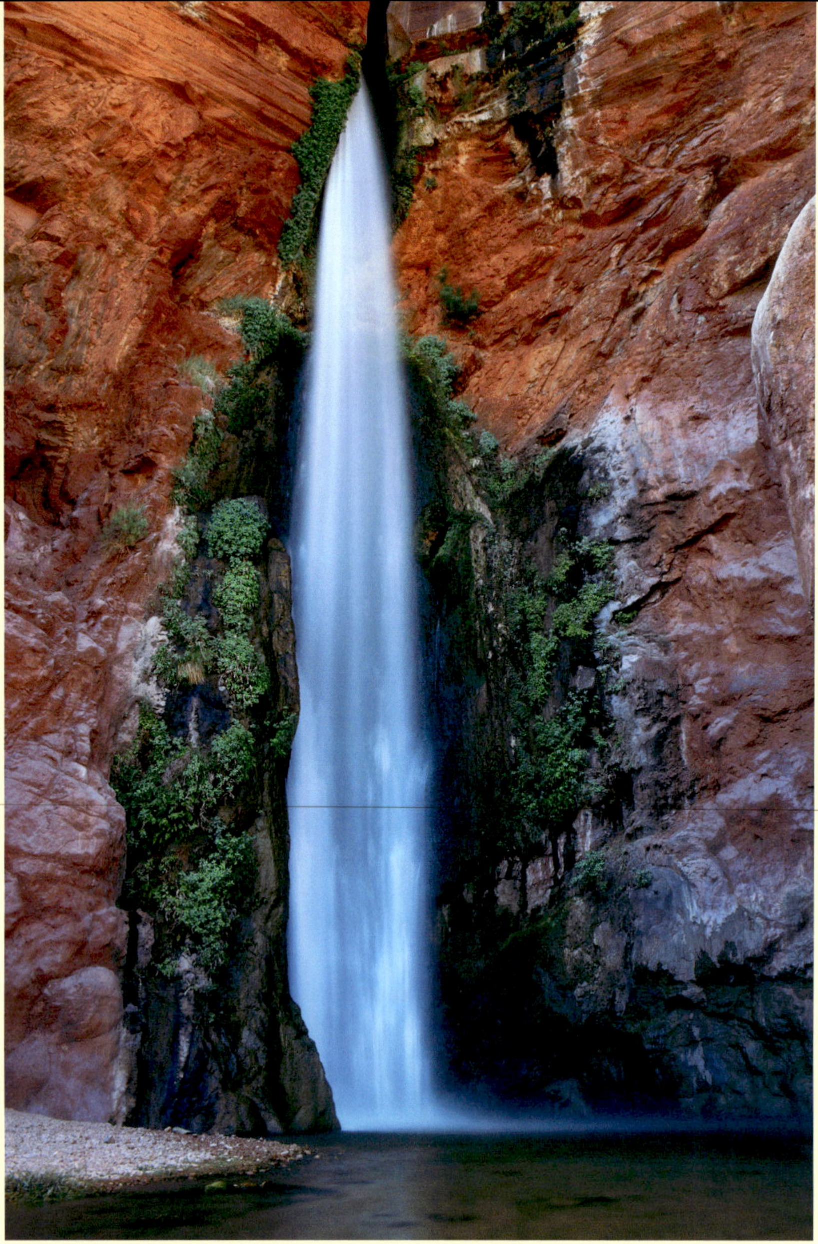

Above: Draining off the Kaibab Plateau, Deer Creek comes to a spectacular end, exiting a slot canyon to plummet more than 180 feet a few dozen yards from the Colorado River at river mile 136.

Right: West of Grand Canyon Village on Hermit Road, the Abyss viewpoint overlooks a sheer drop of 3,000 feet, the largest anywhere on the South Rim.

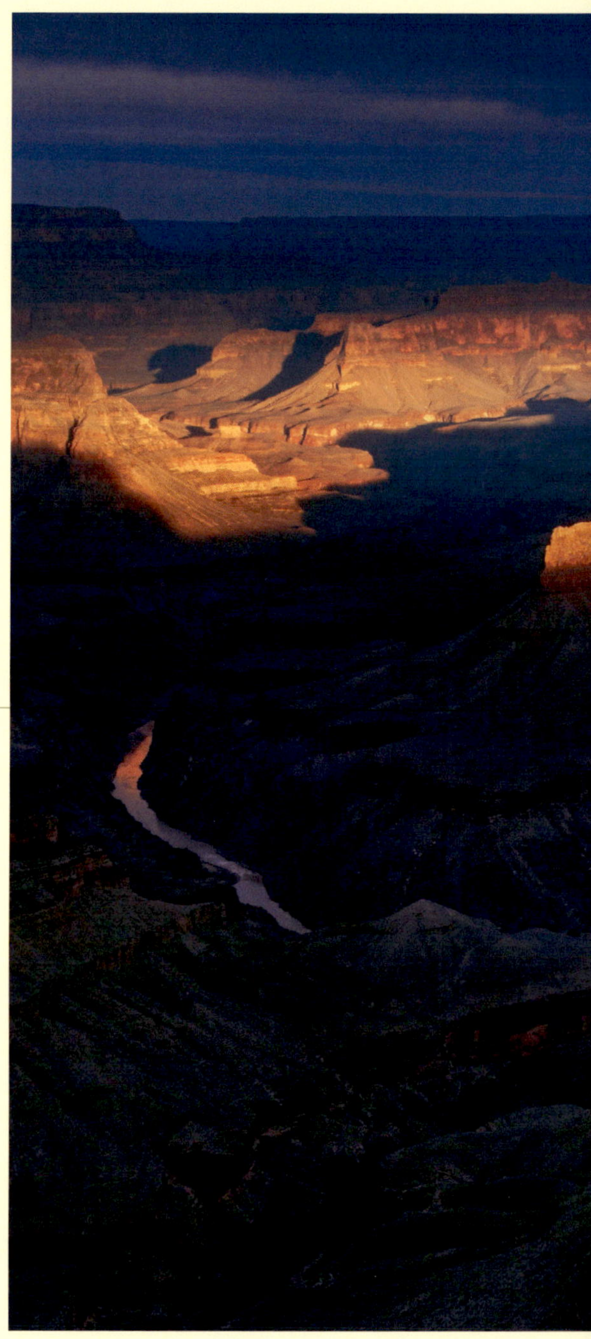

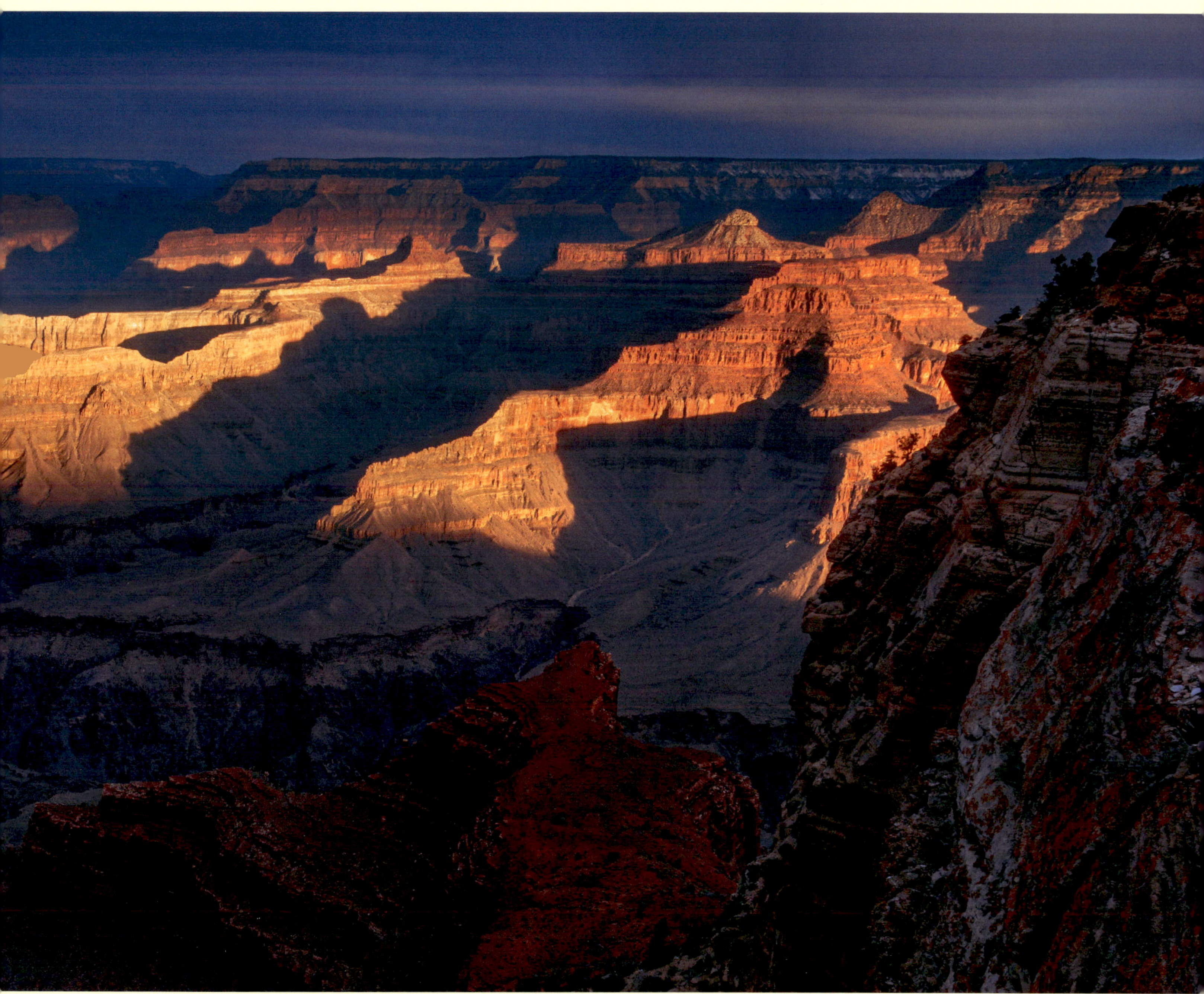

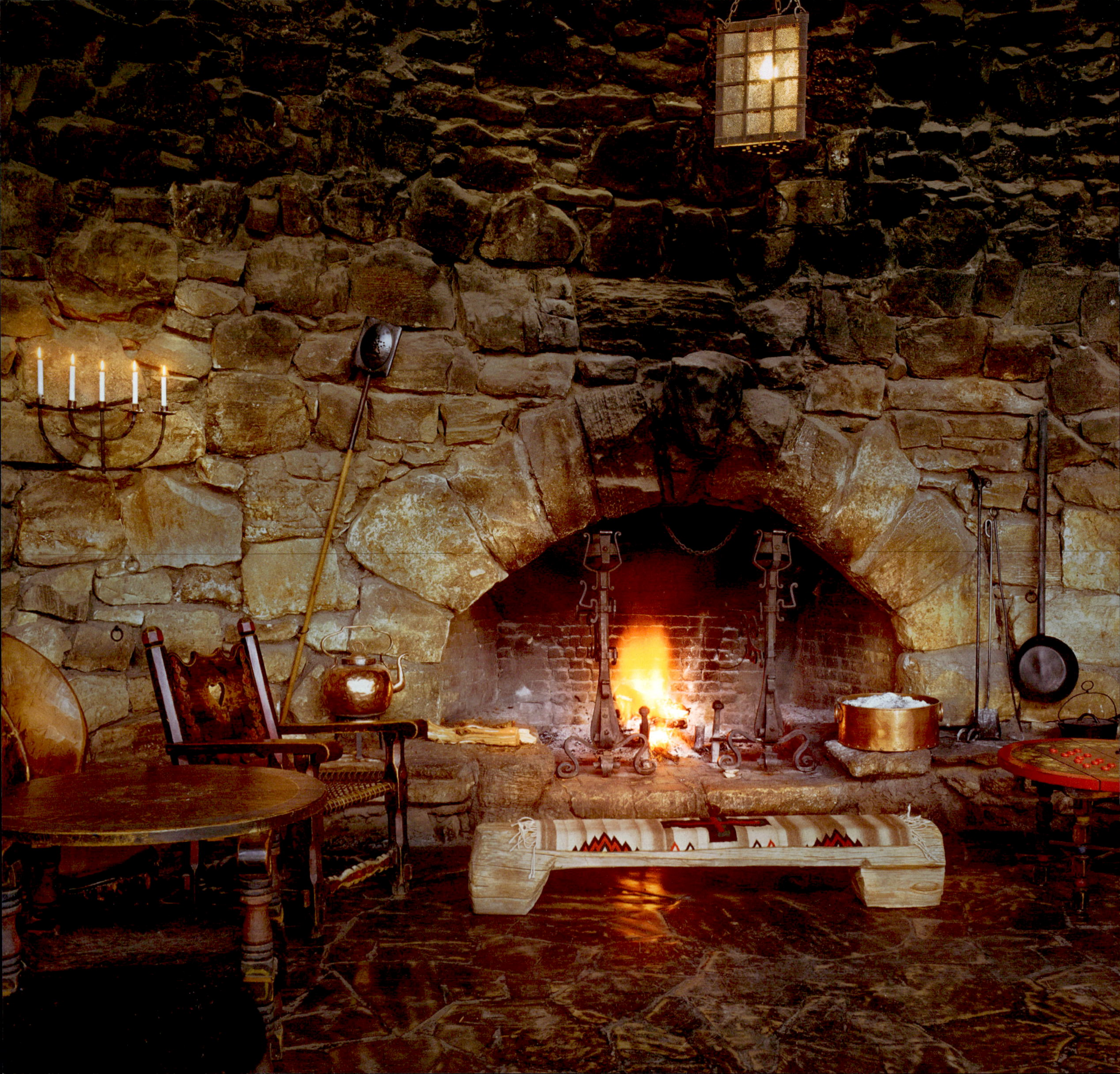

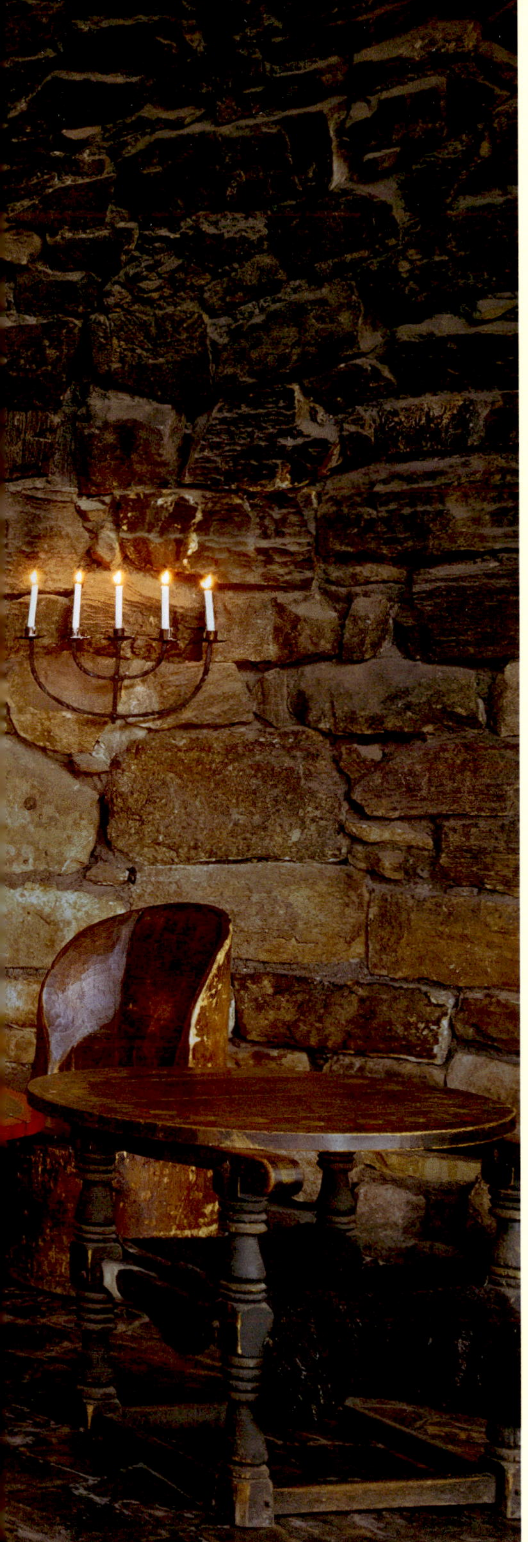

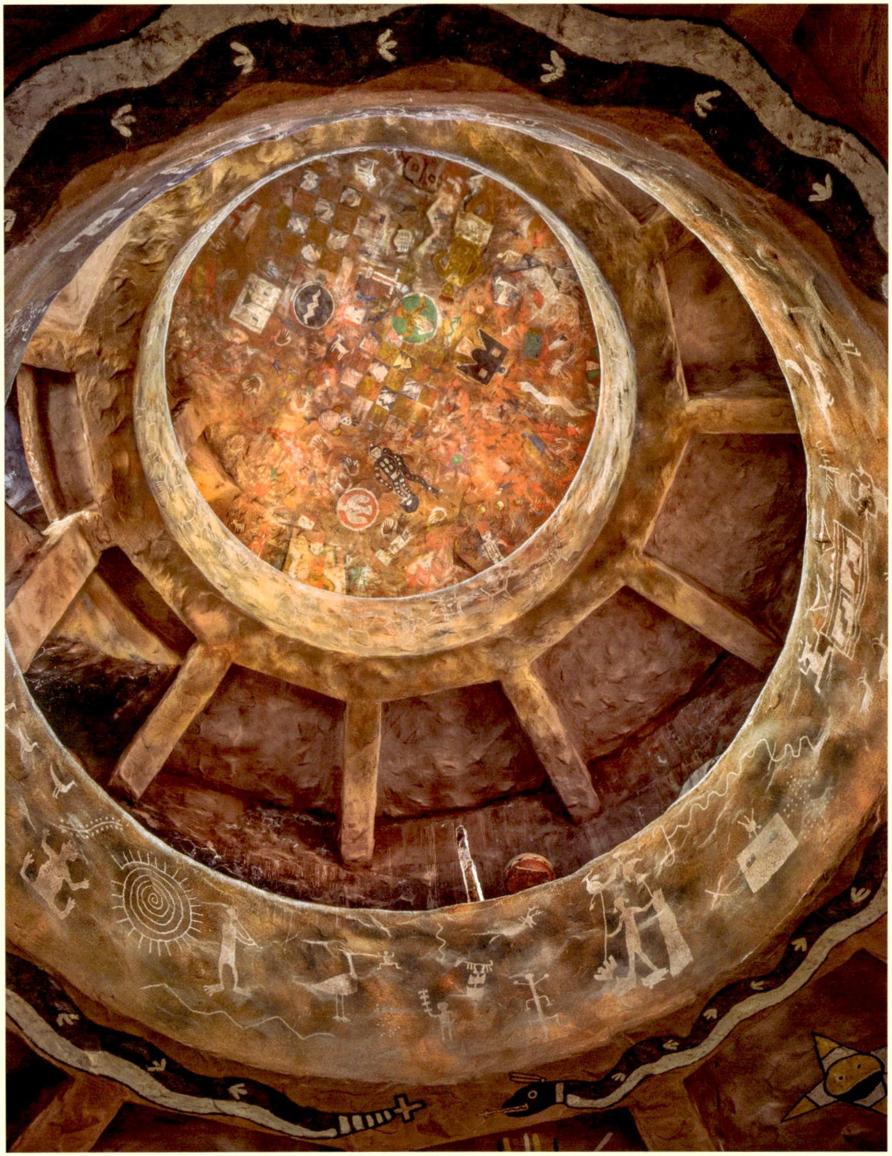

Above: Fred Geary painted this ceiling mural in Desert View Watchtower, with petroglyphs by Hopi artist Chester Dennis on the circular parapet.

Left: Hermit's Rest originally served as a carriage stop at the west end of Hermit Road. Today, the building offers a gift shop and snack bar, and historic charm.

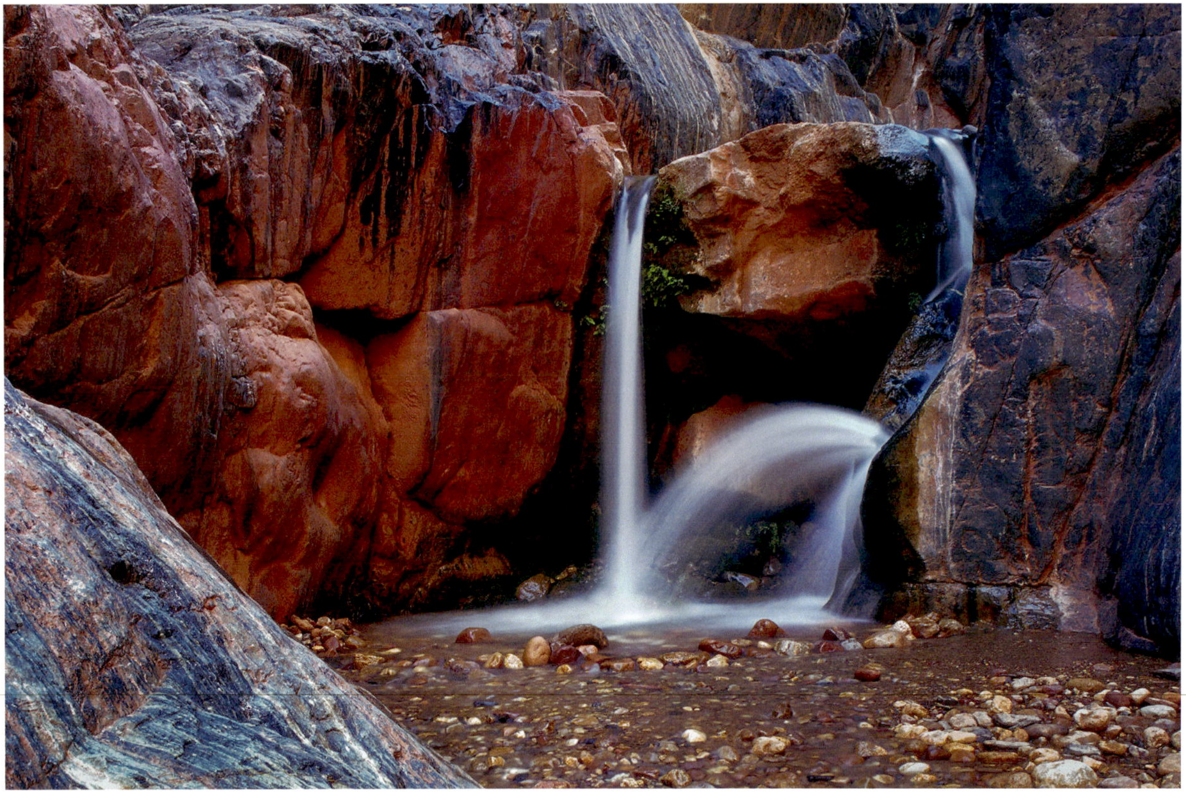

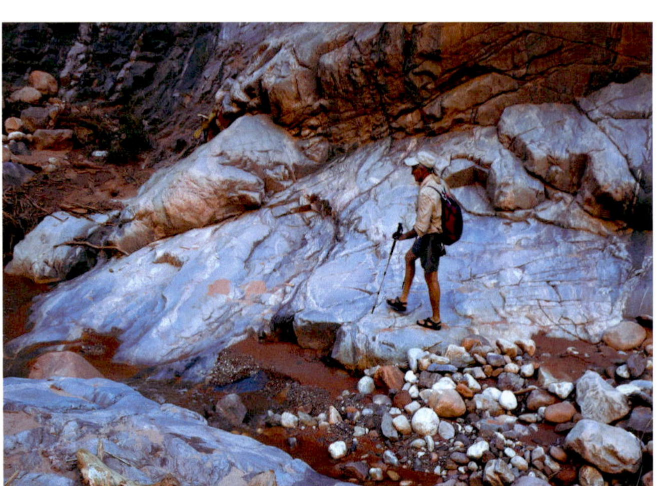

Above: In this landscape where water has long sculpted stone, the elements sometimes playfully reverse roles, as shown here in Clear Creek Canyon.

Right: The narrows of Phantom Creek Canyon offer hours of exploring for intrepid day hikers staying at Phantom Ranch or Bright Angel Campground.

Far right: Backpackers pause to admire the view from a bridge on the Kaibab Trail below the North Rim.

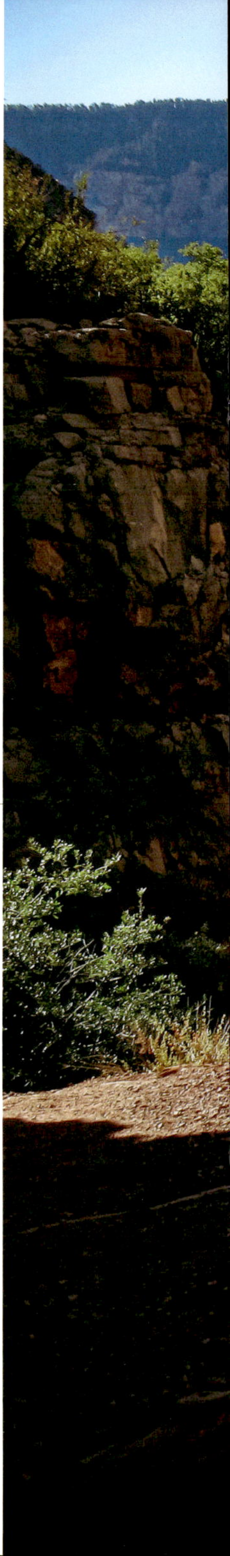

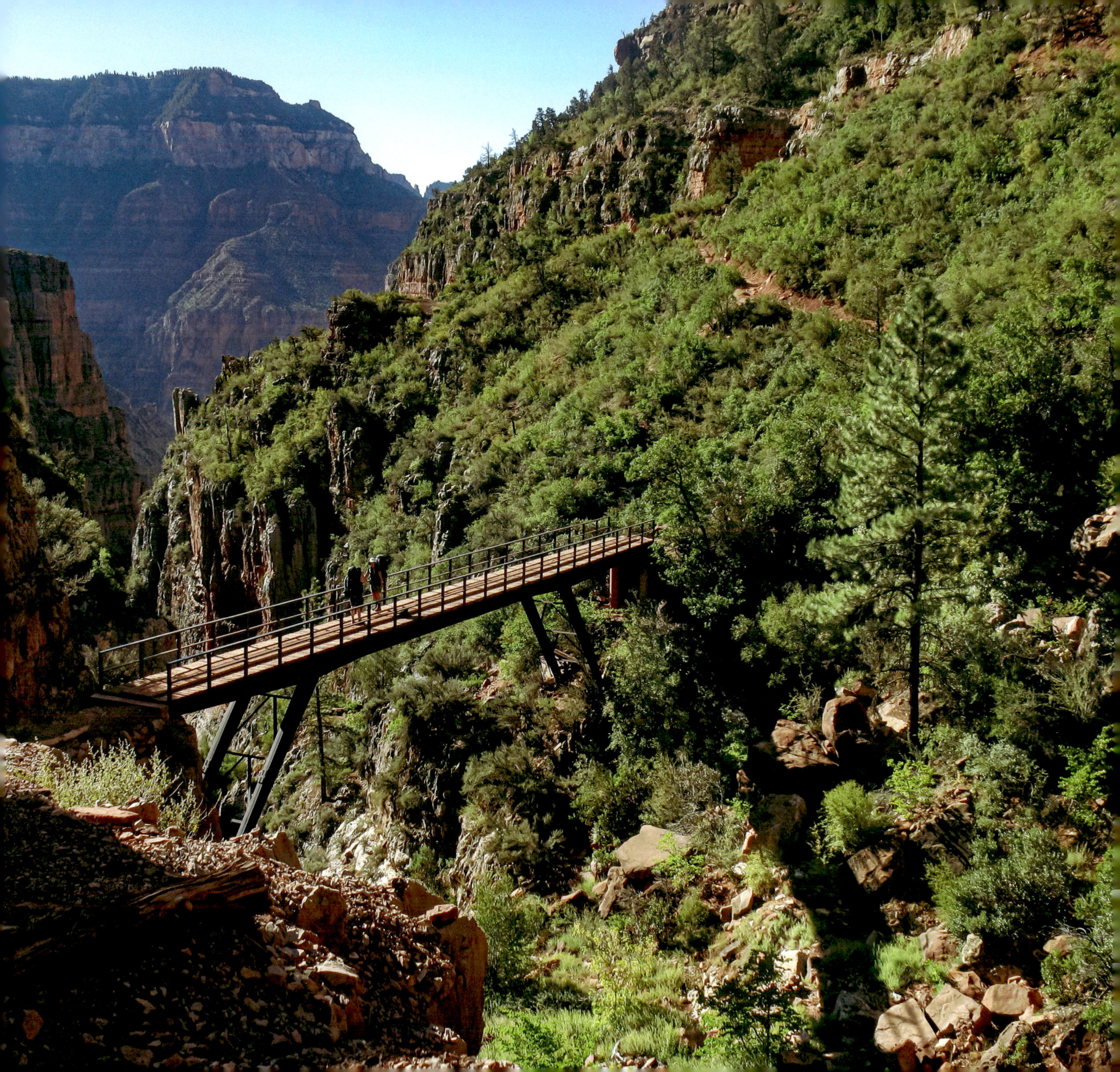

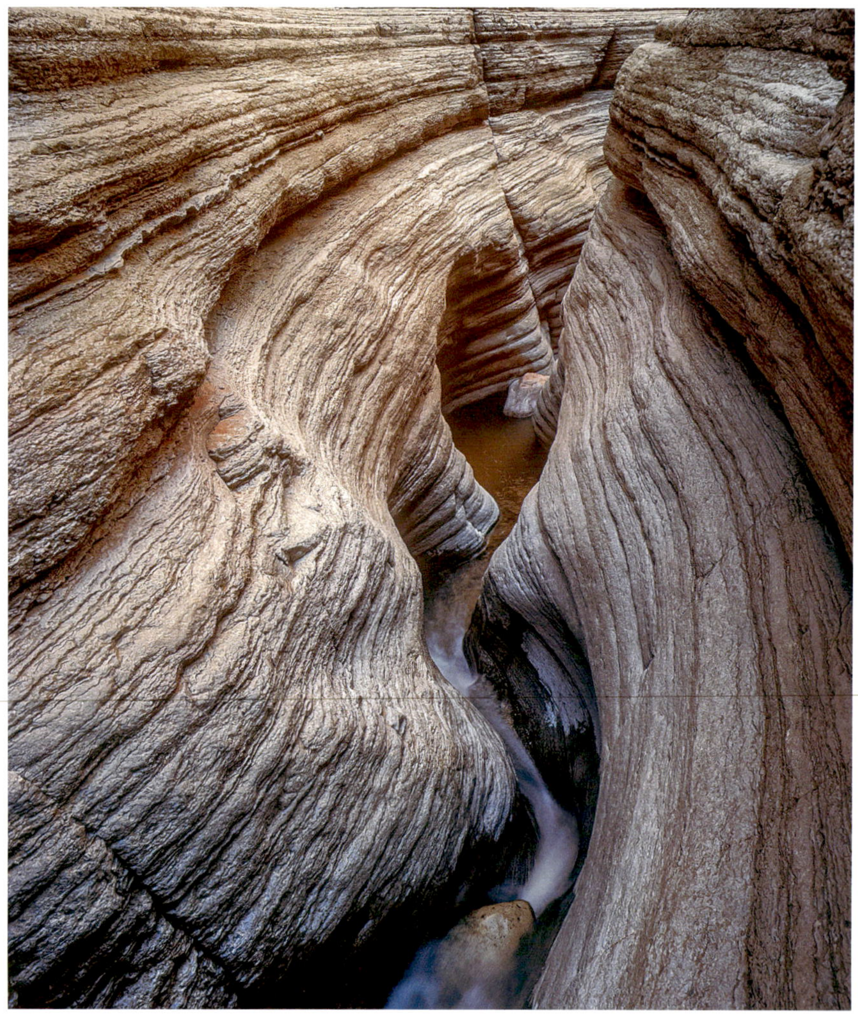

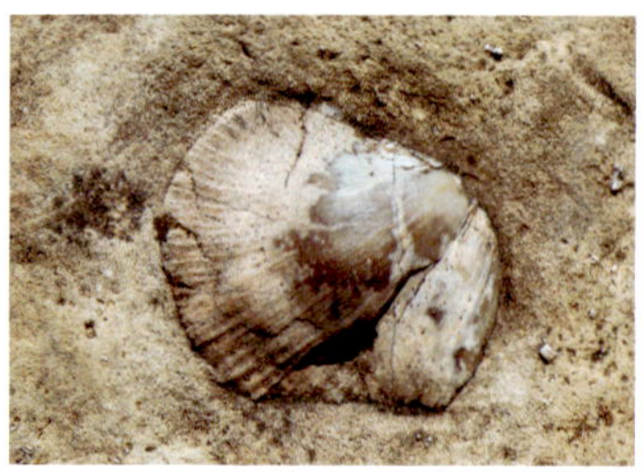

Above: At river mile 148, the narrows of Matkatamiba Canyon cut sinuously through bands of limestone.

Right: Kaibab Limestone harbors a rich diversity of marine fossils, including this bivalve clam shell.

Far right: At Yaki Point, daybreak brings an ever-changing play of light and shadow to a maze of points, buttes, temples, terraces, plateaus, and canyons.

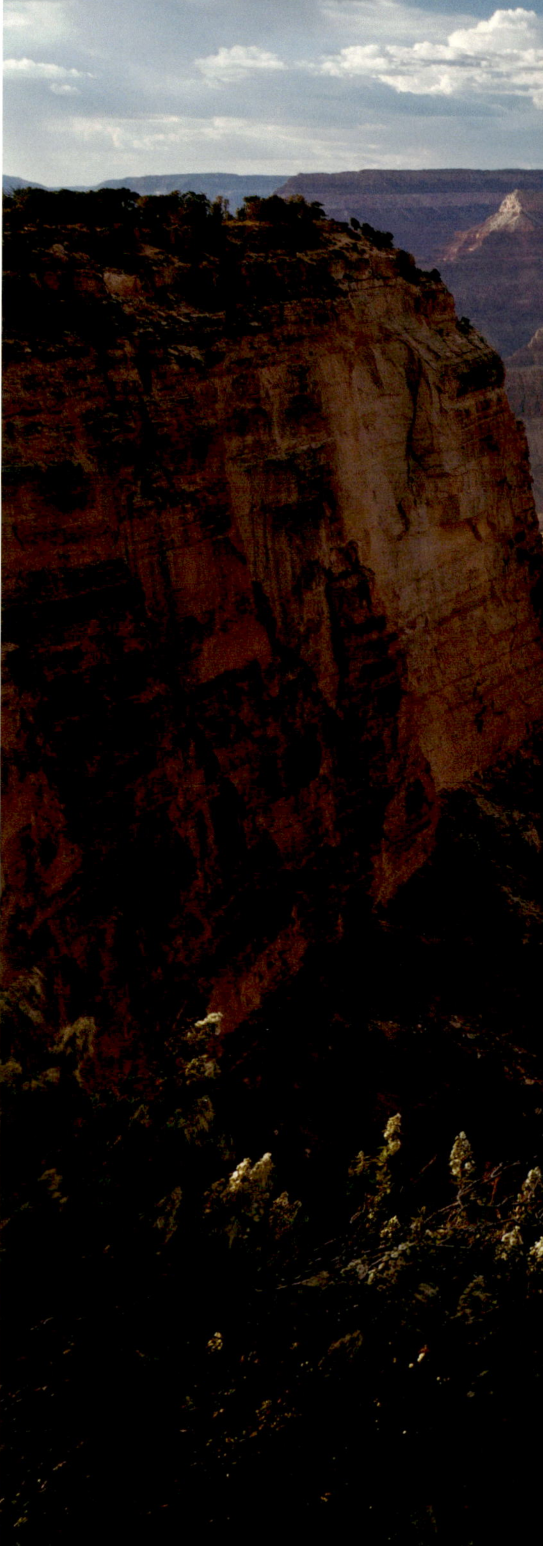

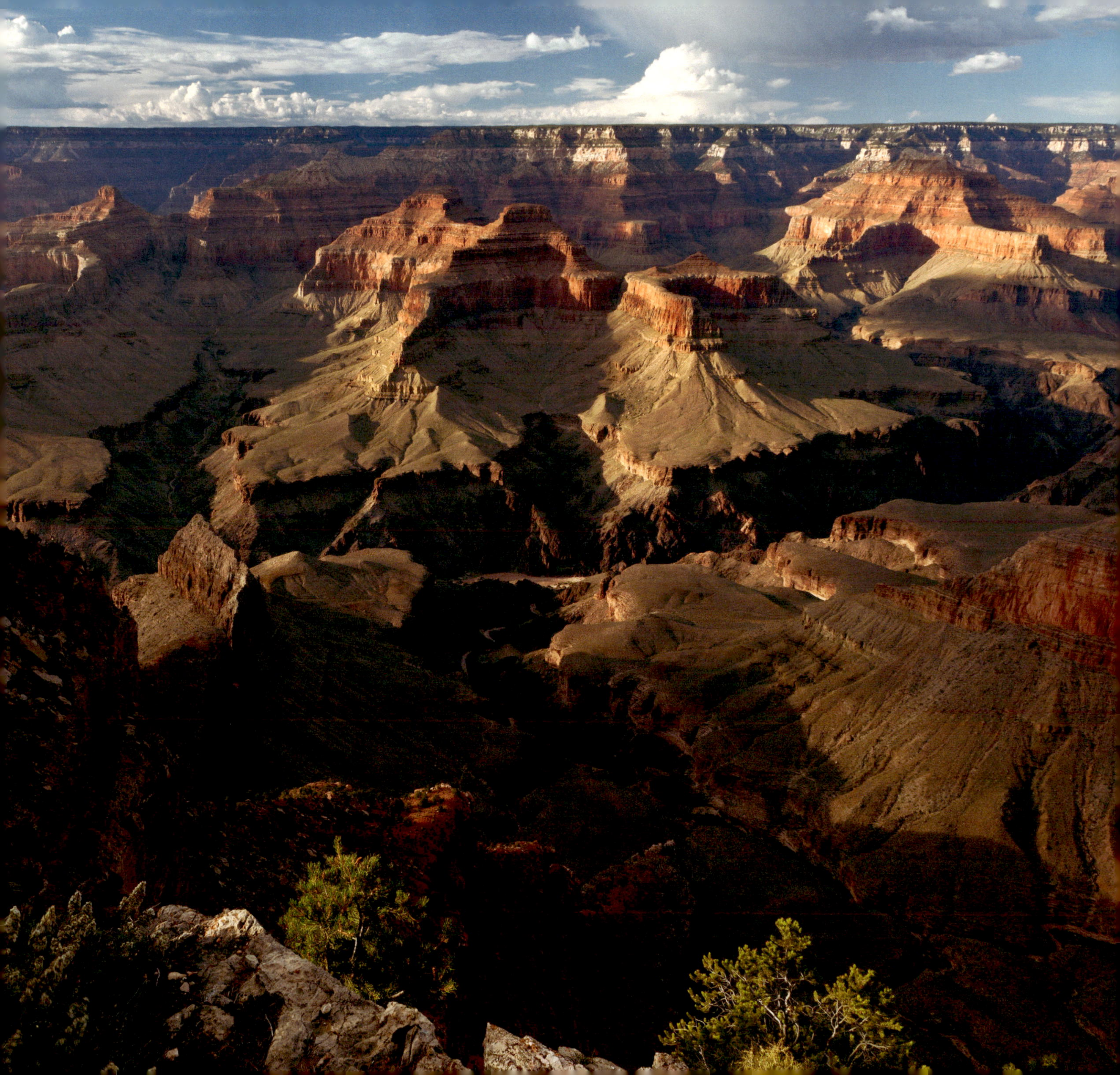

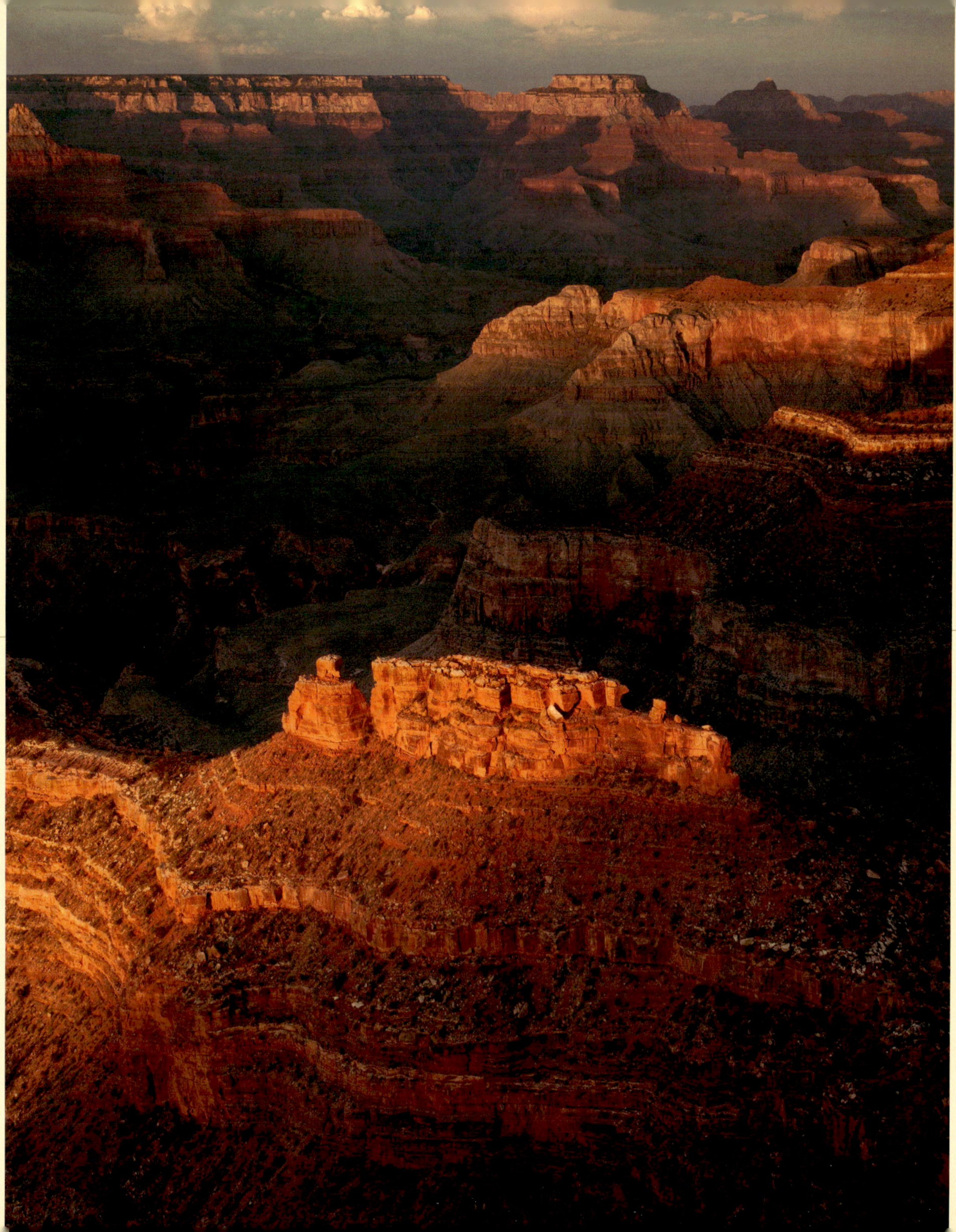

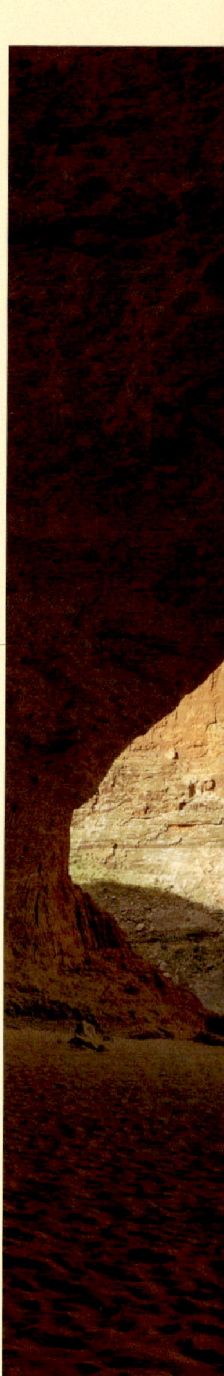

Facing page: From Powell Point, sunset burnishes the Battleship in the foreground.

Below: At river mile 33, immense Redwall Cavern showcases the power of high-water currents and time.

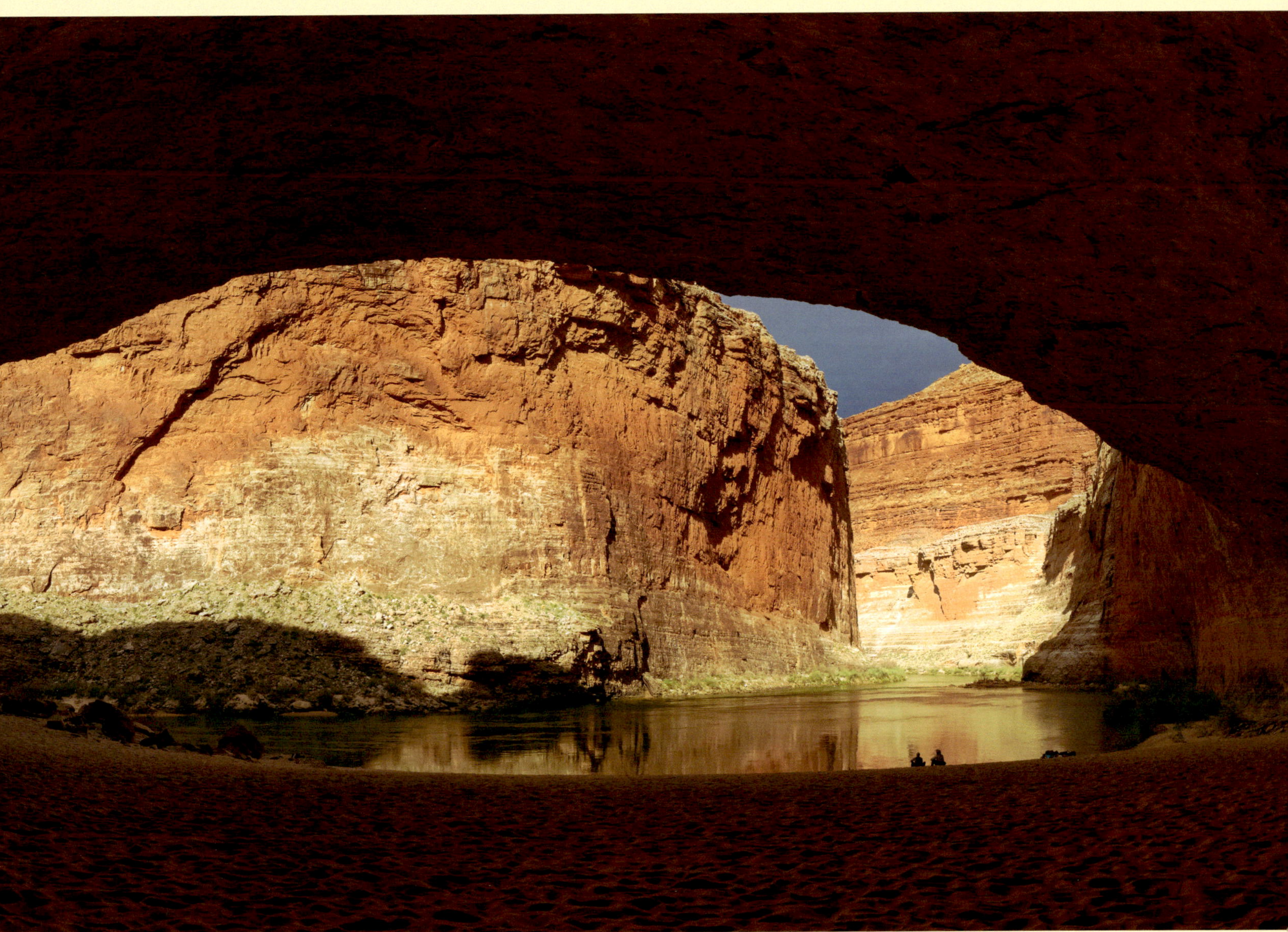

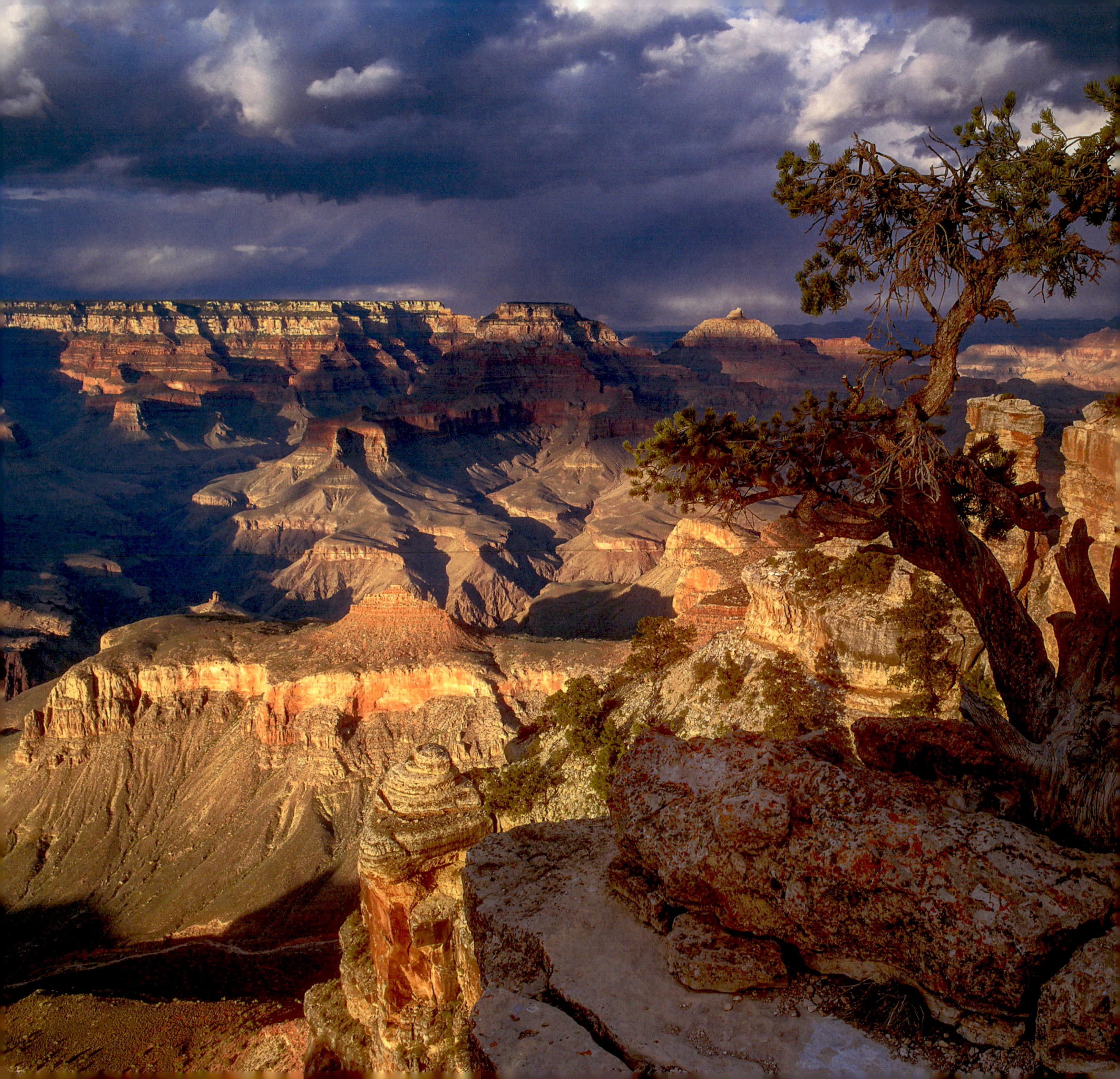

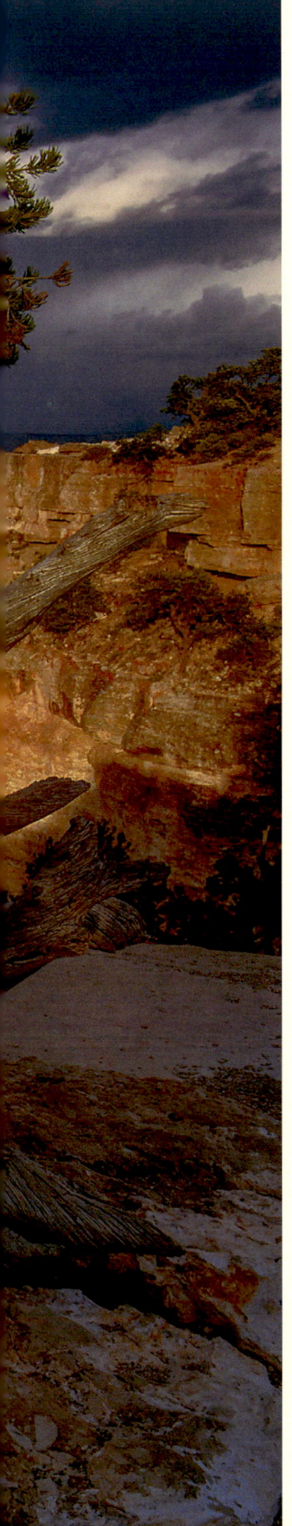

Left: A weathered pinyon pine serves as sentinel to the close of another day at Yaki Point on the South Rim.

Below: Historic Bright Angel Lodge, designed in 1935, continues to welcome guests with rustic architecture and rim-side lodging in the heart of Grand Canyon Village.

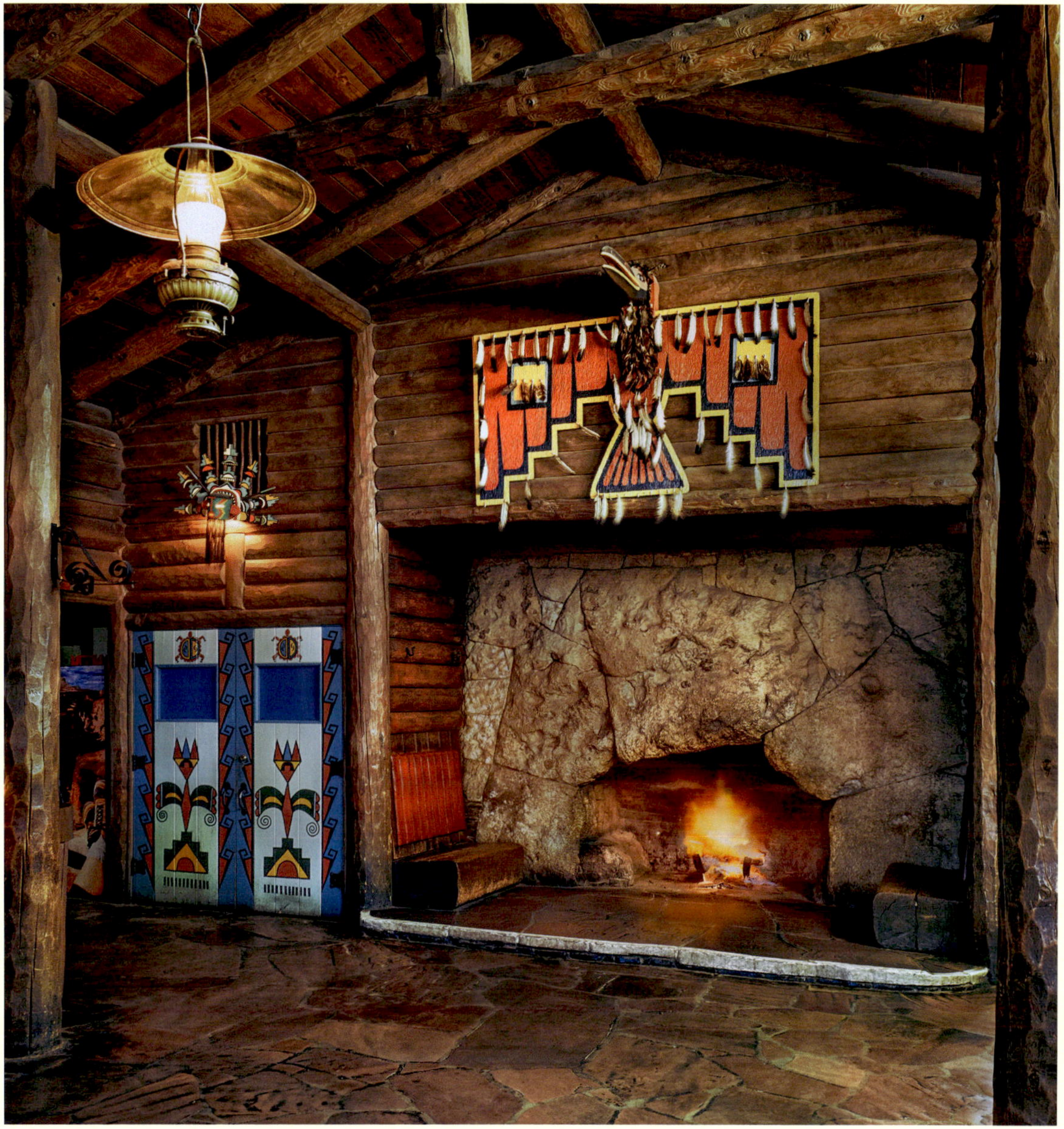

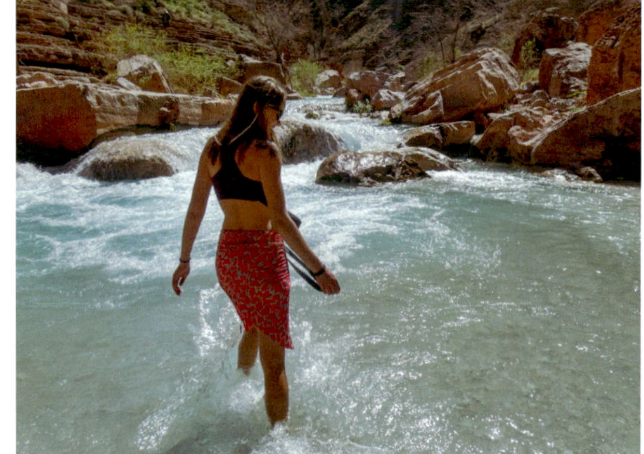

Right: Havasu Creek meets the Colorado River at river mile 157, luring passing boaters to wade in its milky turquoise waters.

Far right: From a high ledge at river mile 29, rafts on the Colorado bring a sense of scale to the towering canyon walls and ribbon of river.

Below: A cataraft navigates Crystal Rapid at river mile 98.2.

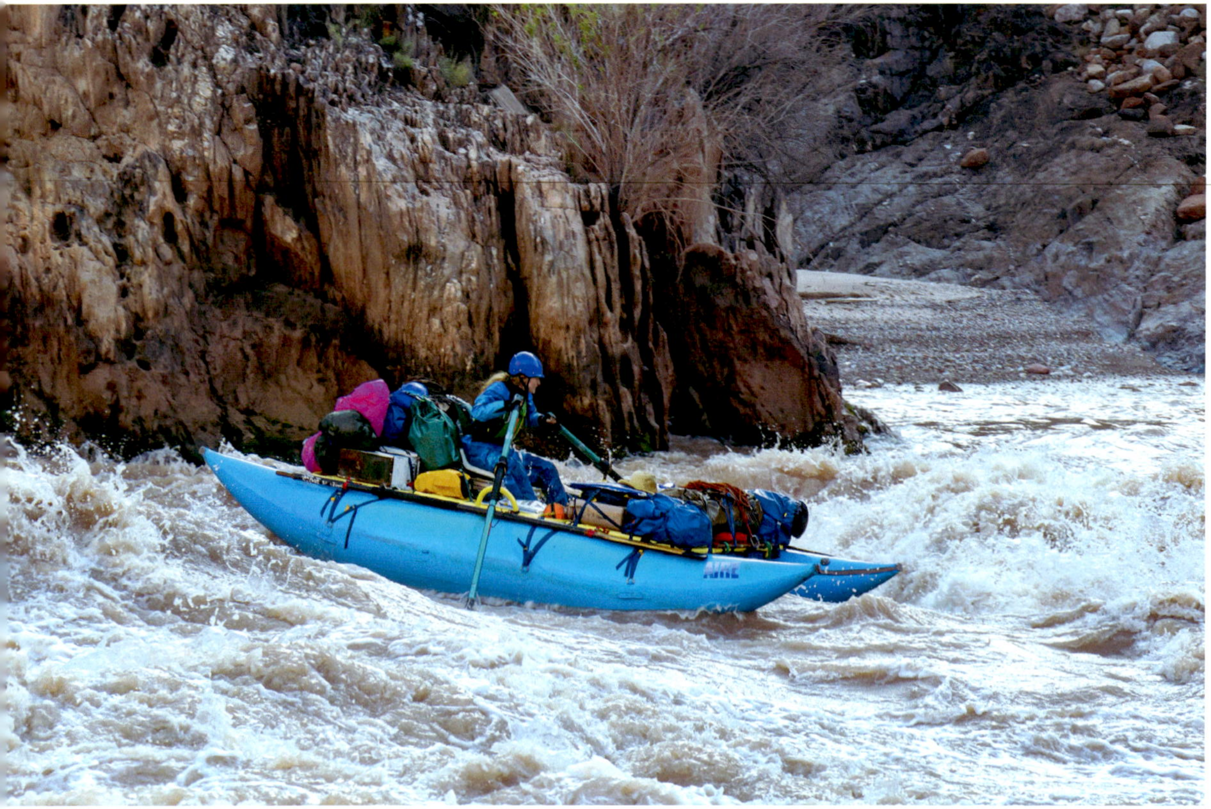

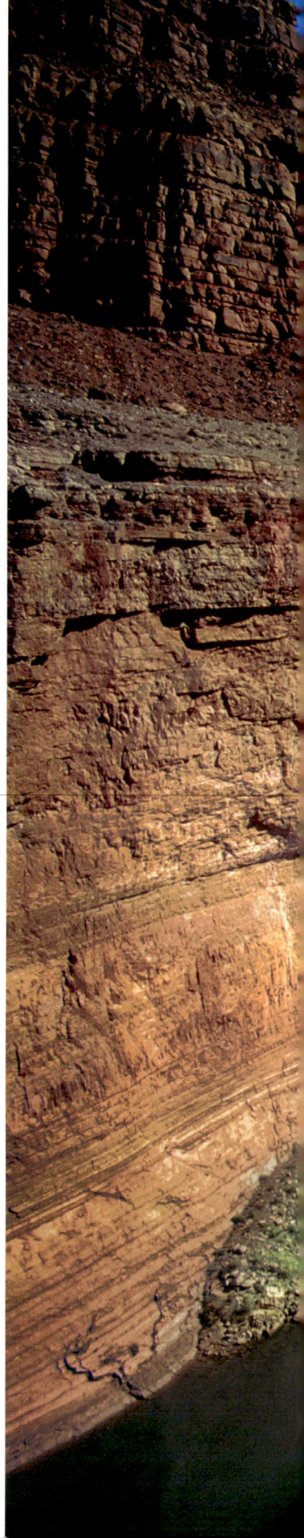

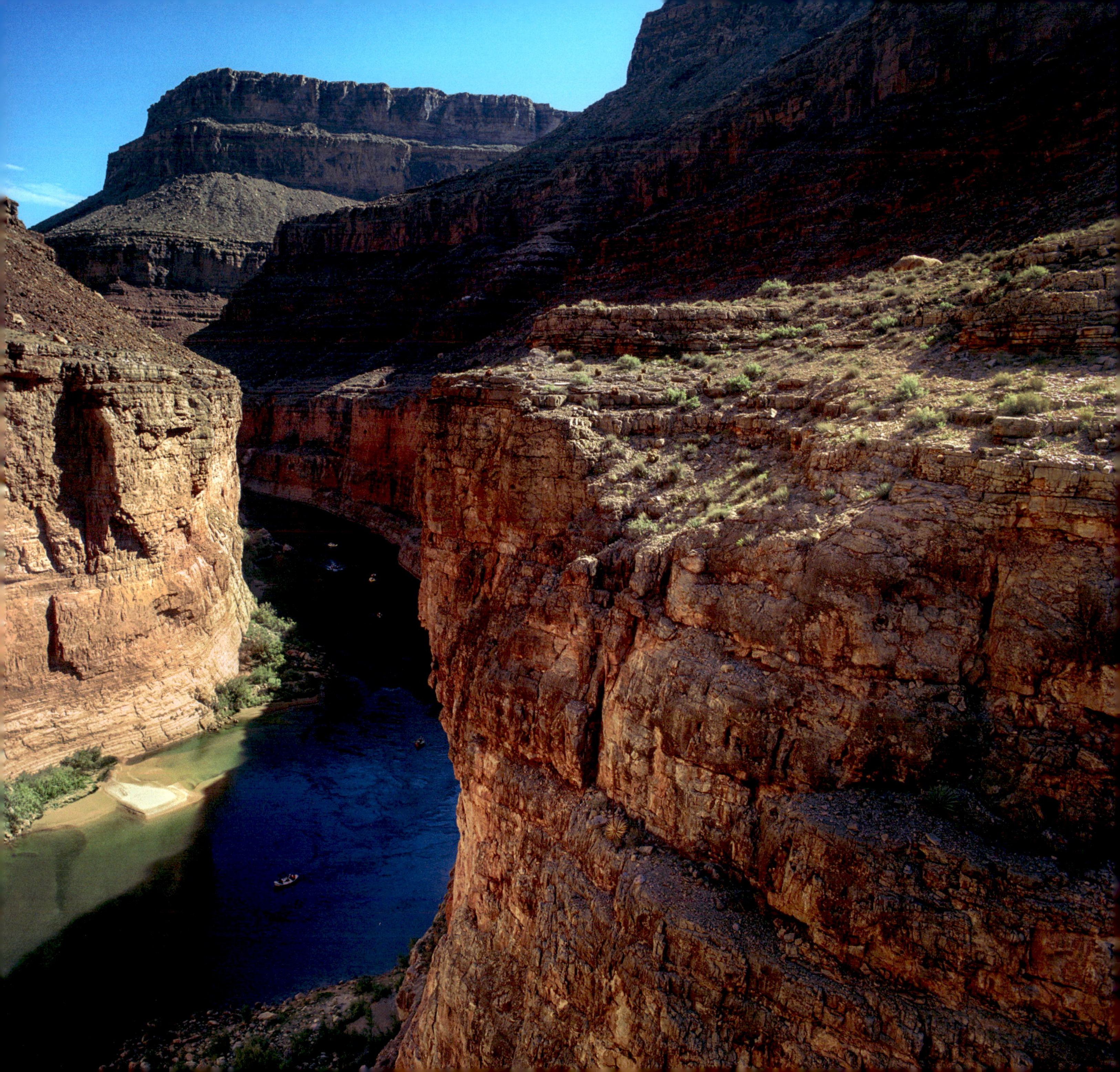

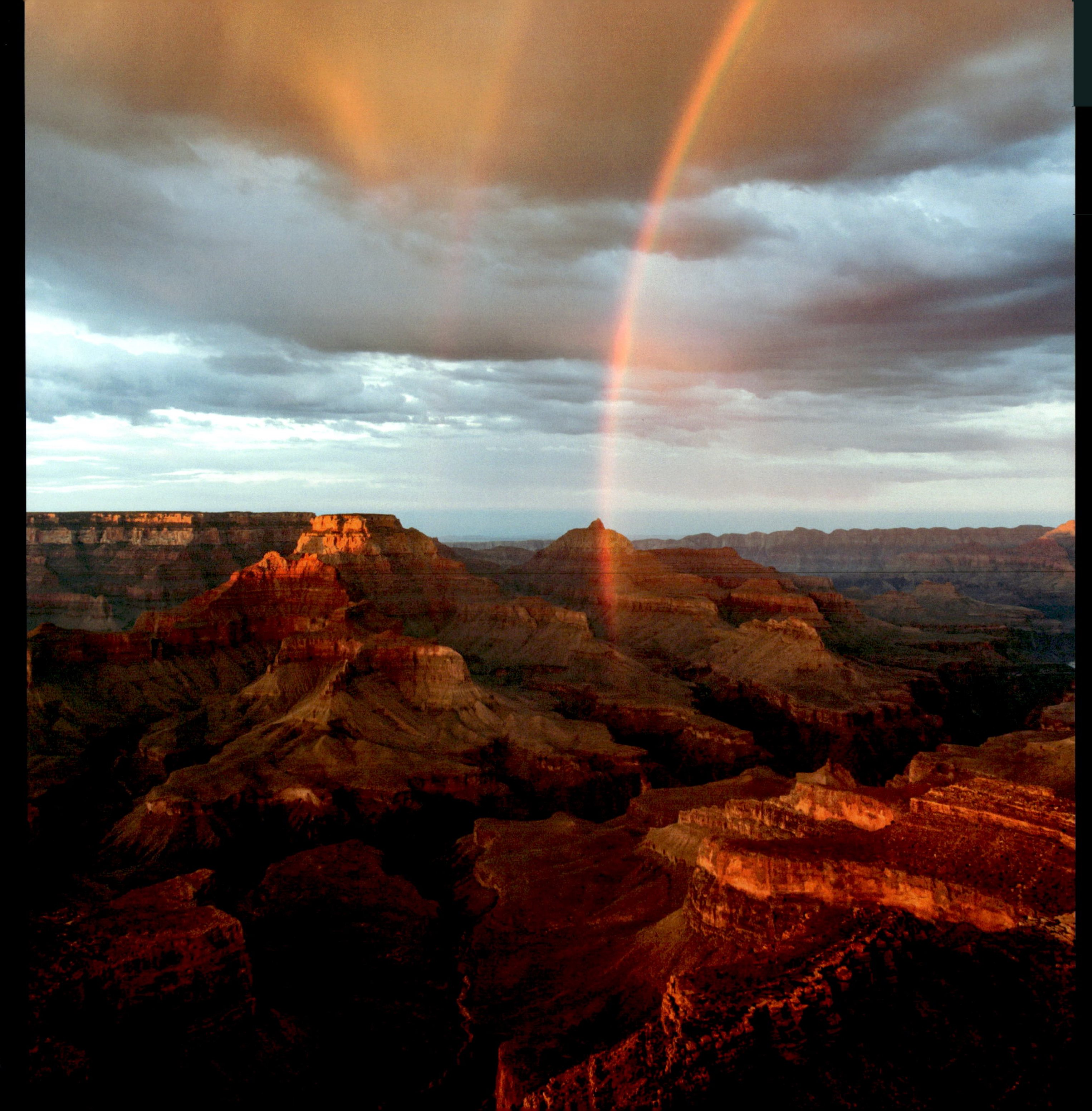

Facing page: At Shoshone Point on the South Rim, a double rainbow scythes into the canyon over Vishnu Temple.

Below: Sunrise burnishes land and sky at Navajo Point.

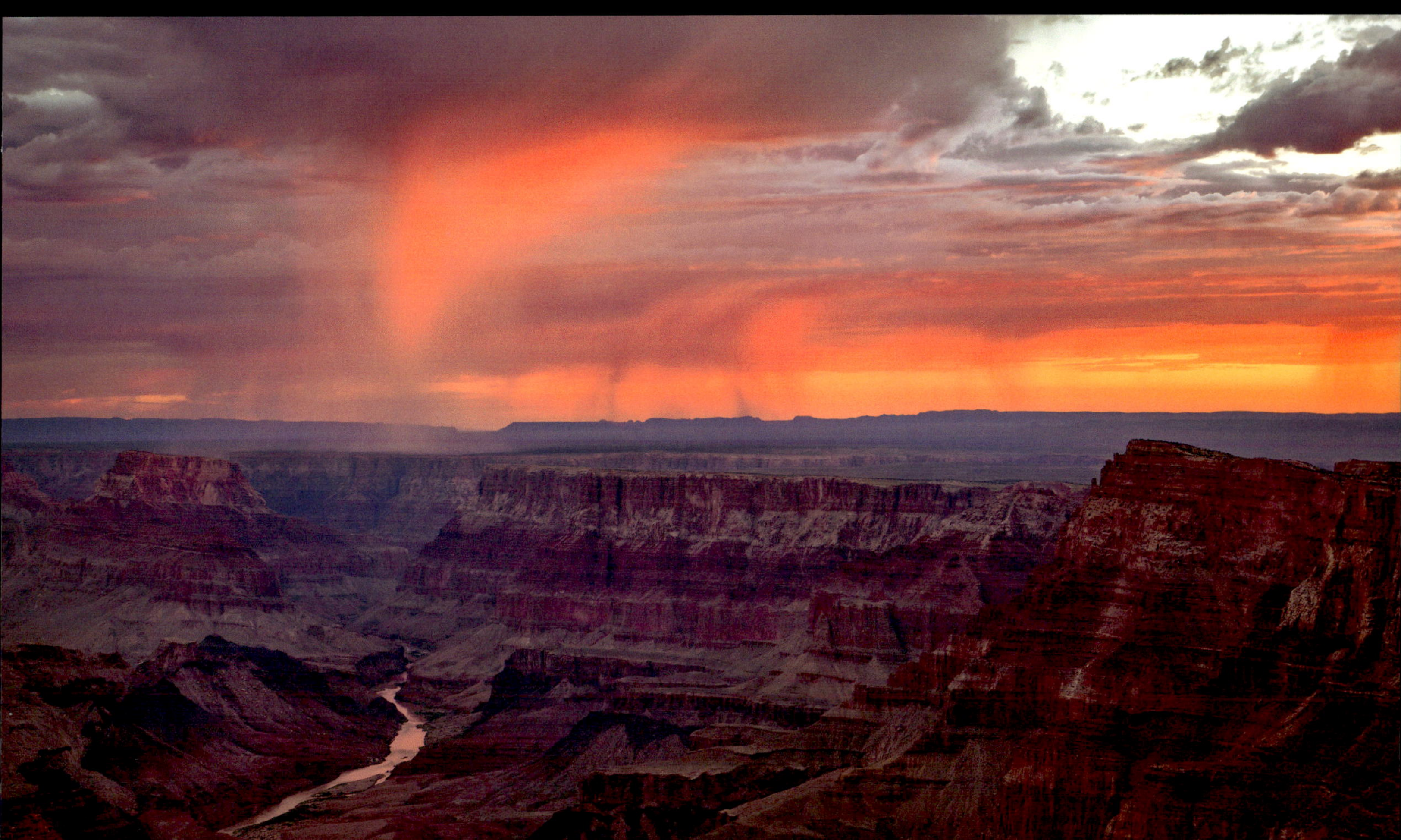

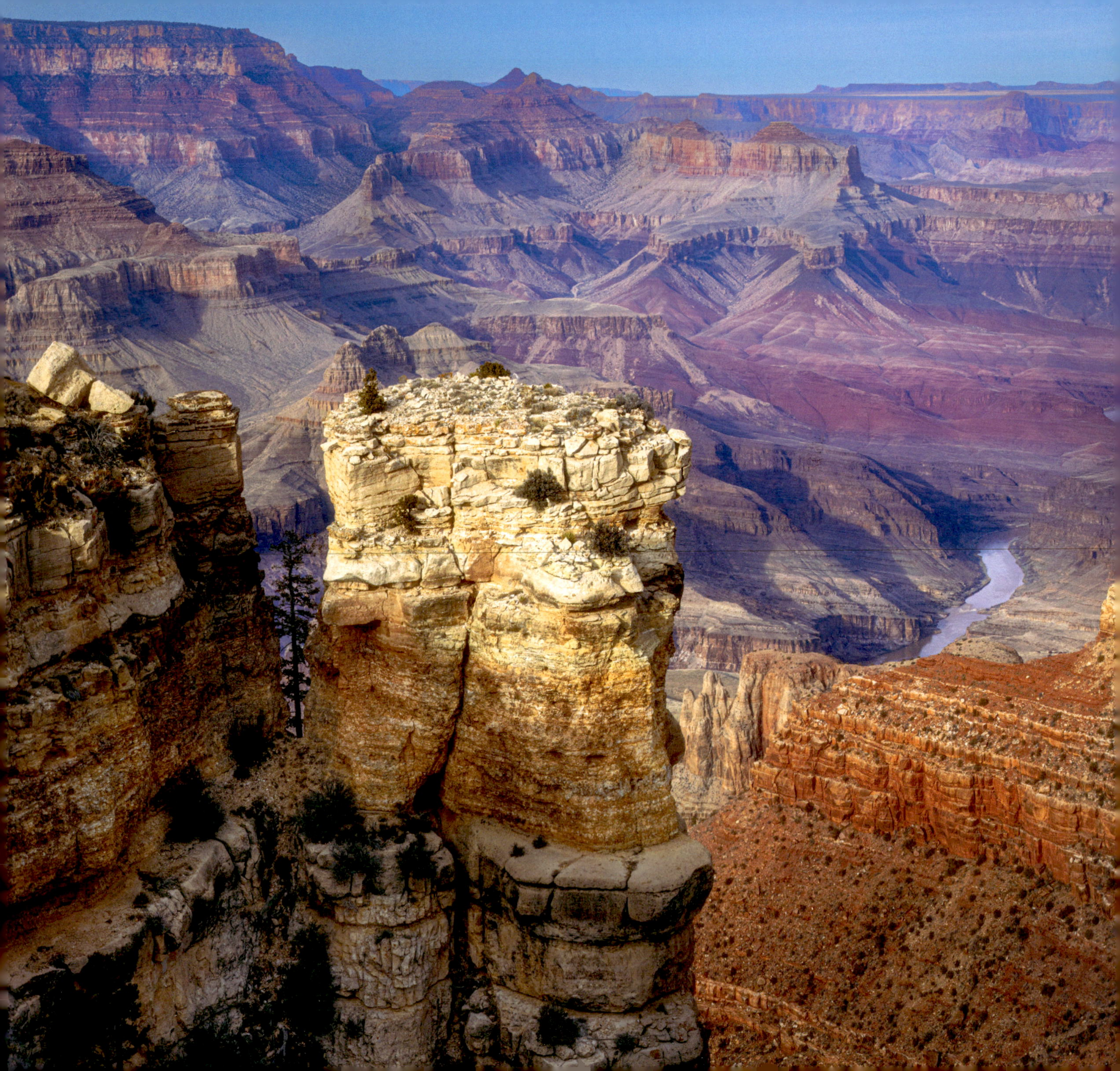

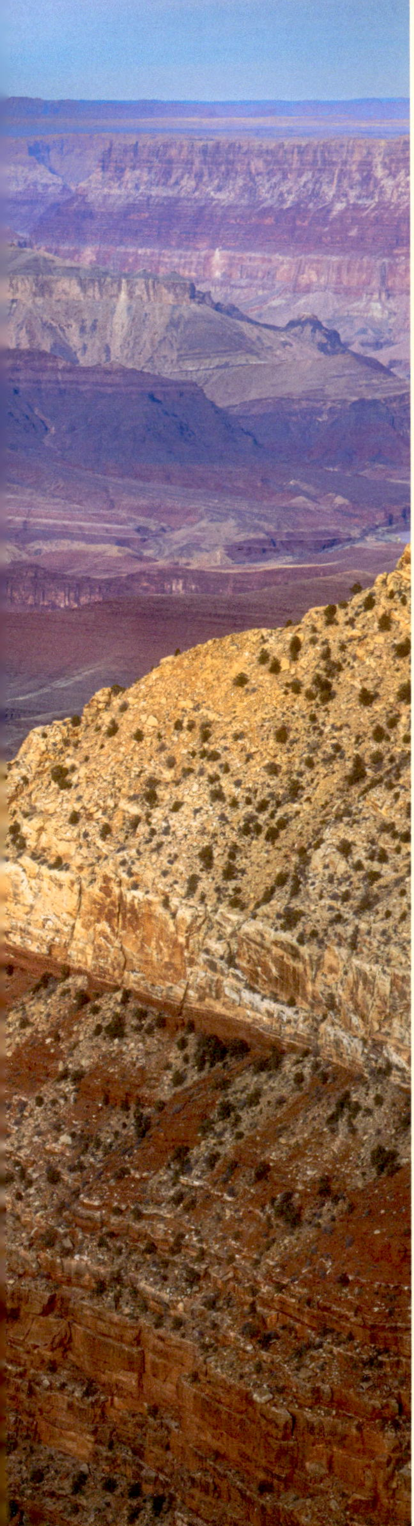

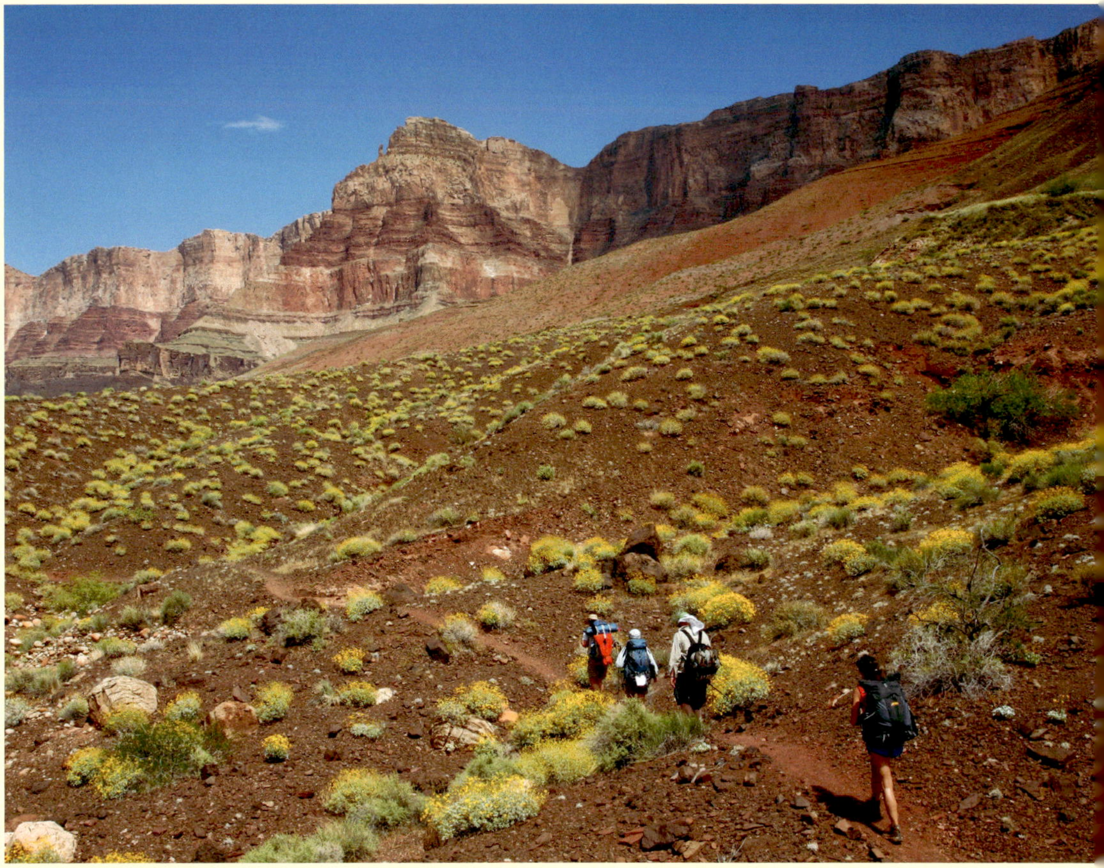

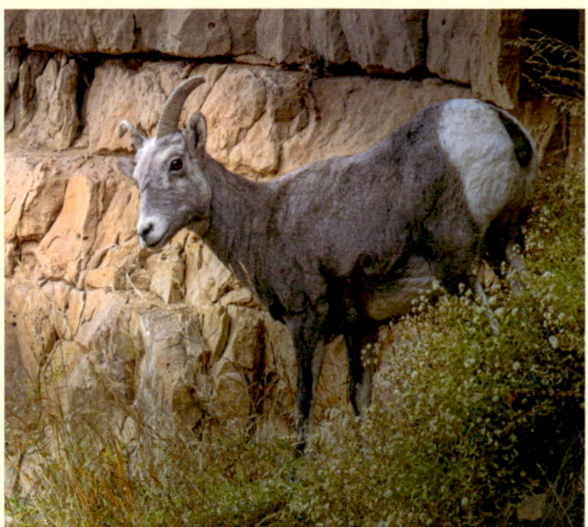

Above: Hikers traverse a slope of brittle brush on the climb toward the South Rim.

Left: Desert bighorn sheep are well adapted to the cliffy terrain of the canyon.

Far left: Moran Point offers views of the canyon's multi-hued layers.

Right: The claretcup is a species of hedgehog cactus that thrives in the sandy soils of the Grand Canyon.

Far right: A wall at Toroweap Point greets the morning sun high above the Colorado River.

Below: Clear-running Kwagunt Creek is named after a notable nineteenth-century leader of the Southern Paiutes.

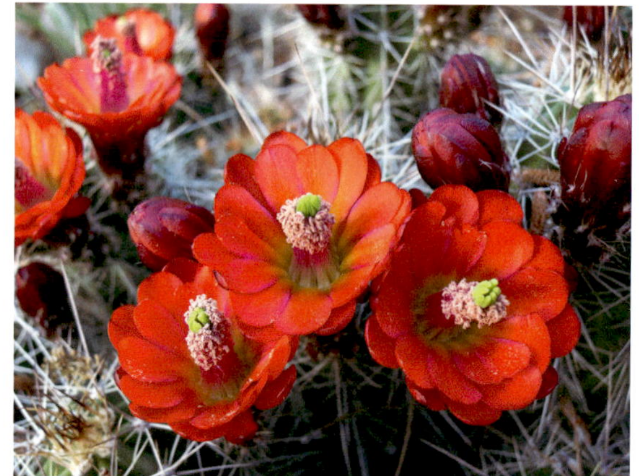

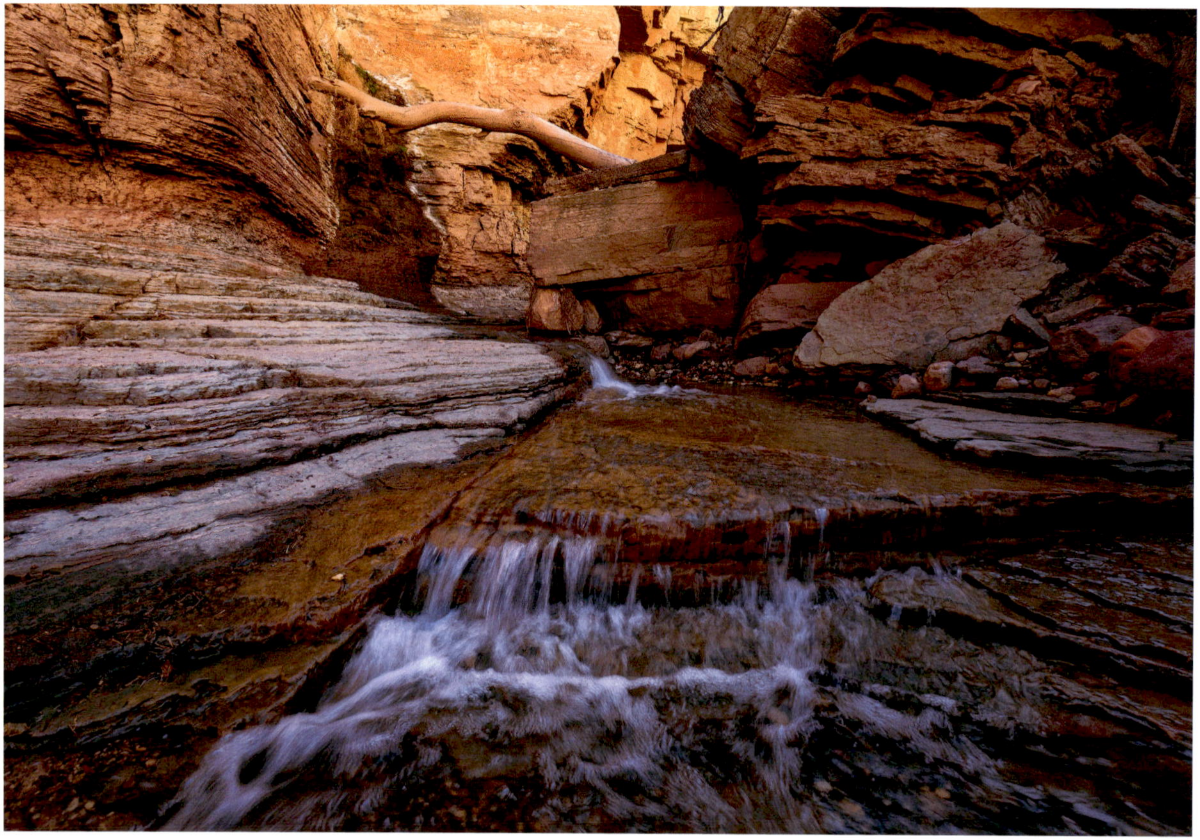

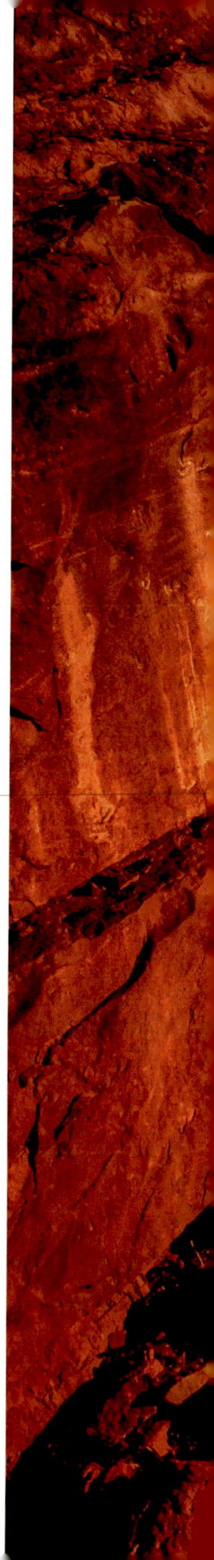

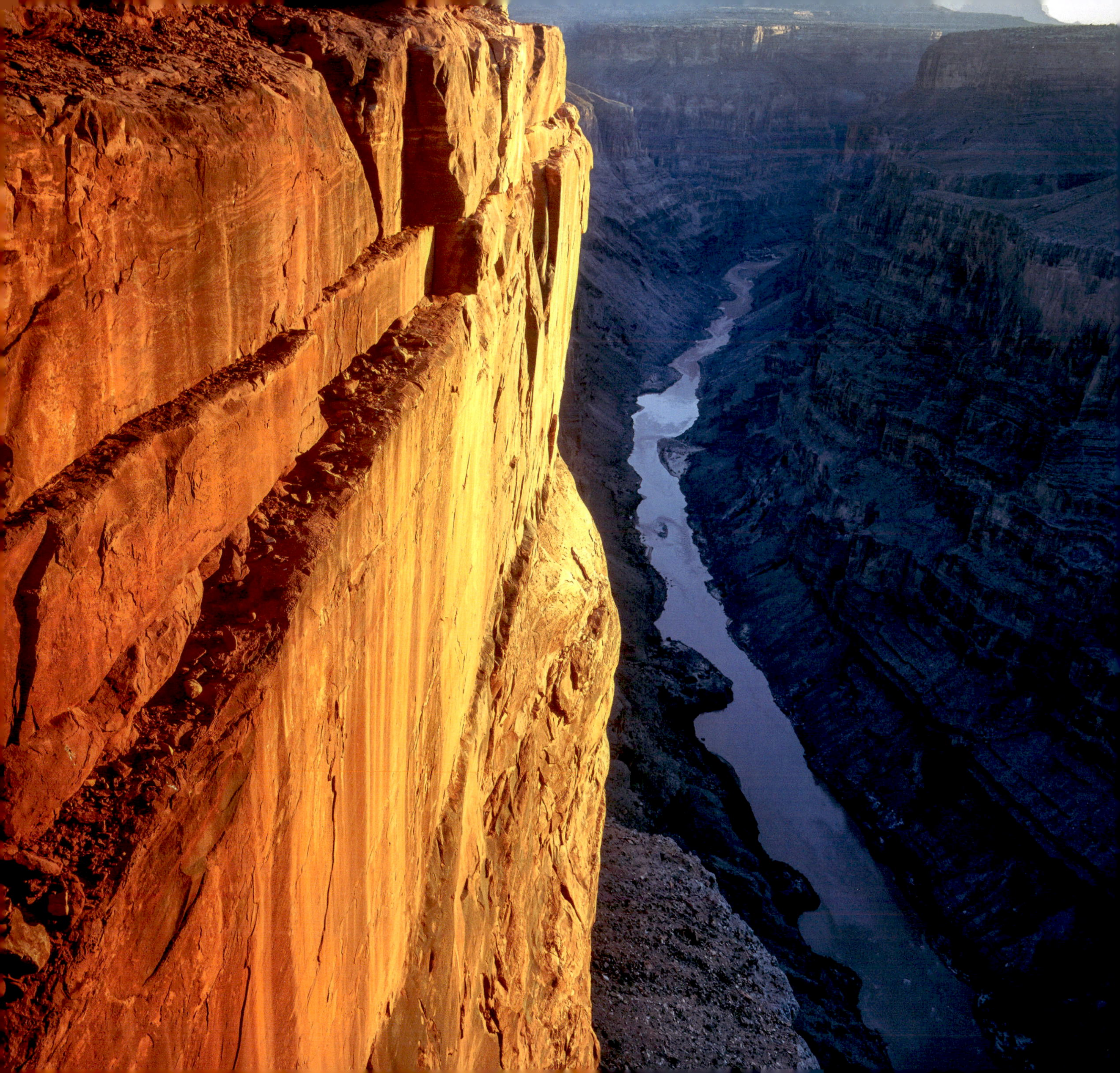

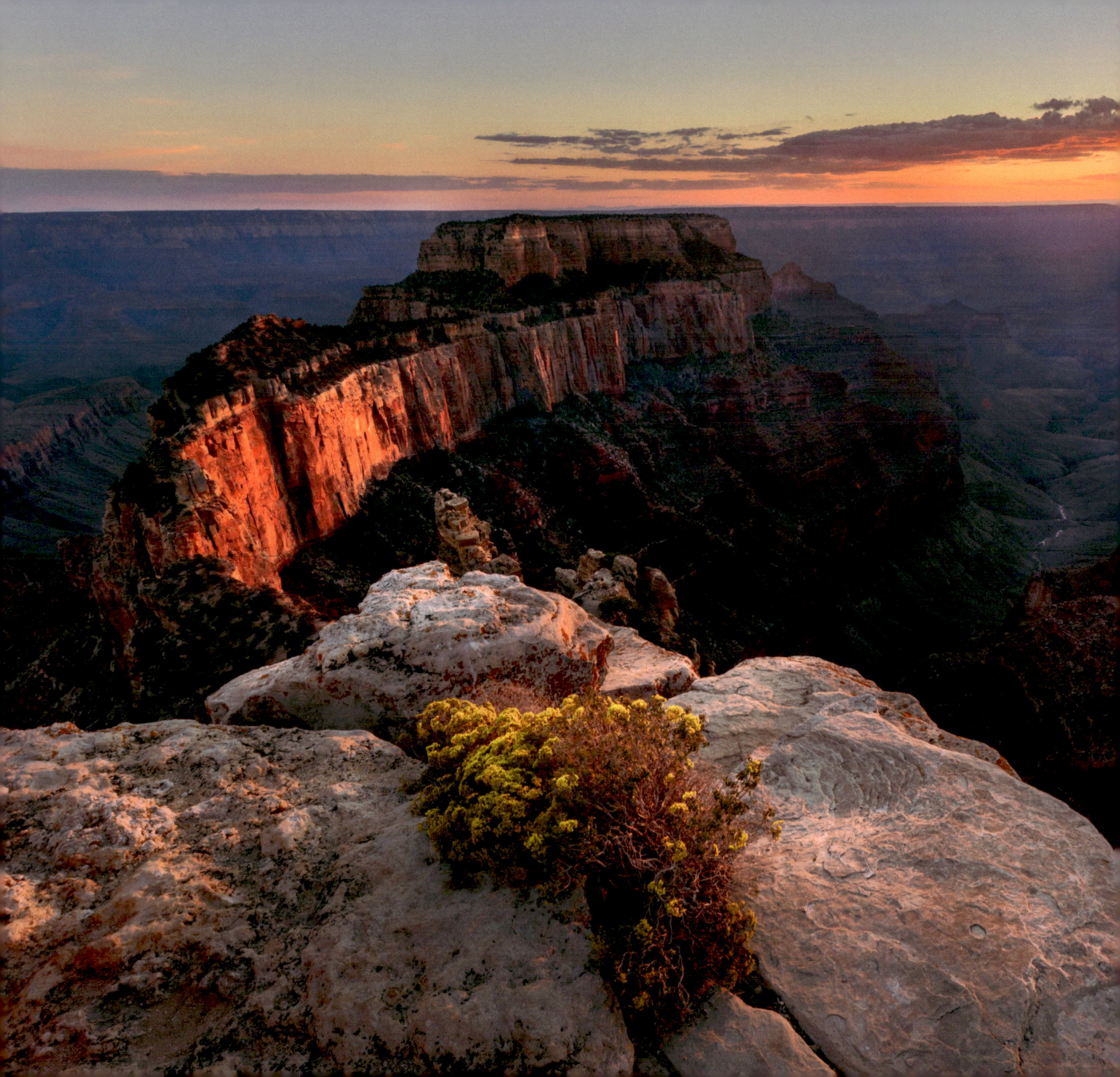

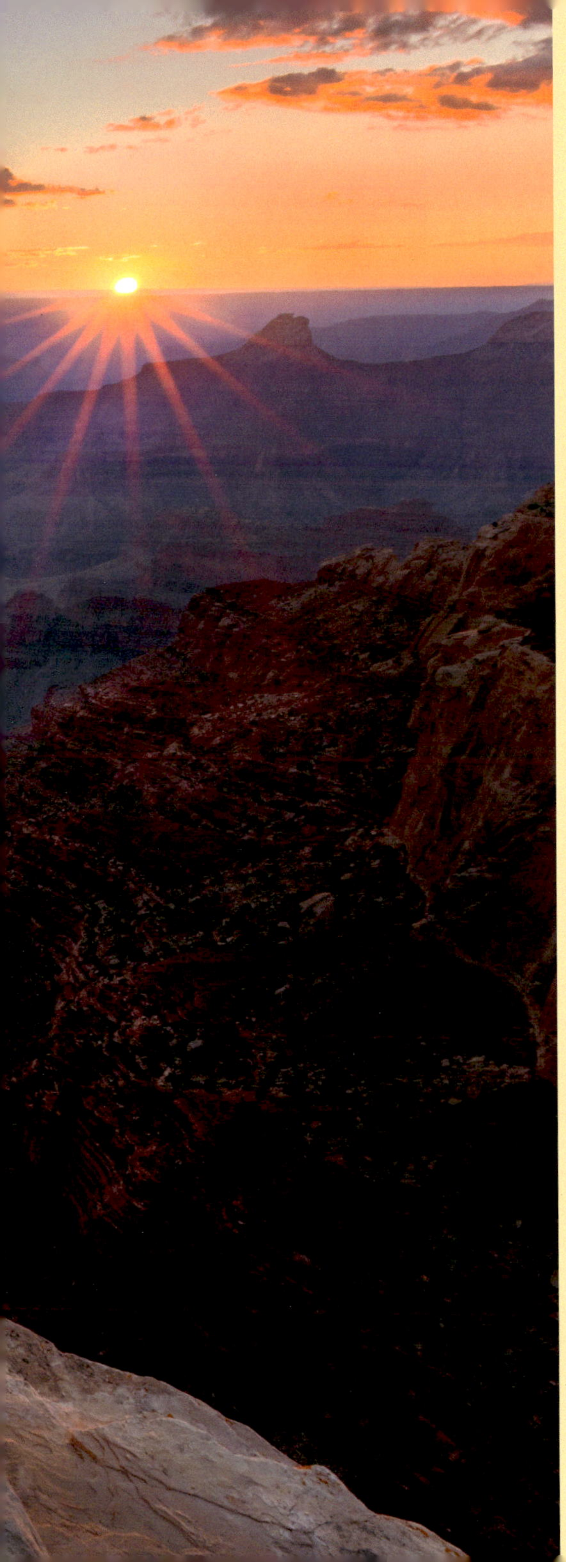

Left: The silver thread of Clear Creek glistens below Wotans Throne, as seen from Cape Royal on the North Rim.

Below: Grasses, moss, and other plants flourish in the microclimate created by Upper Ribbon Falls.

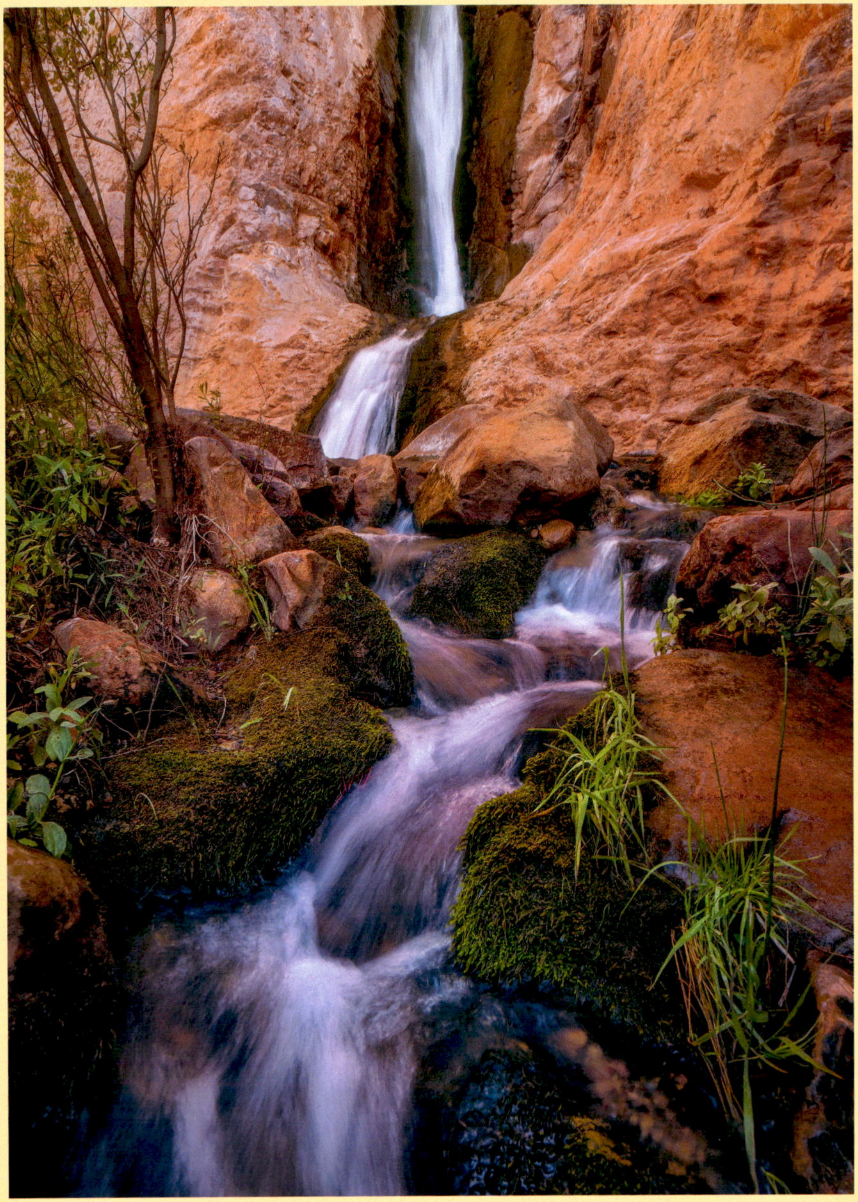

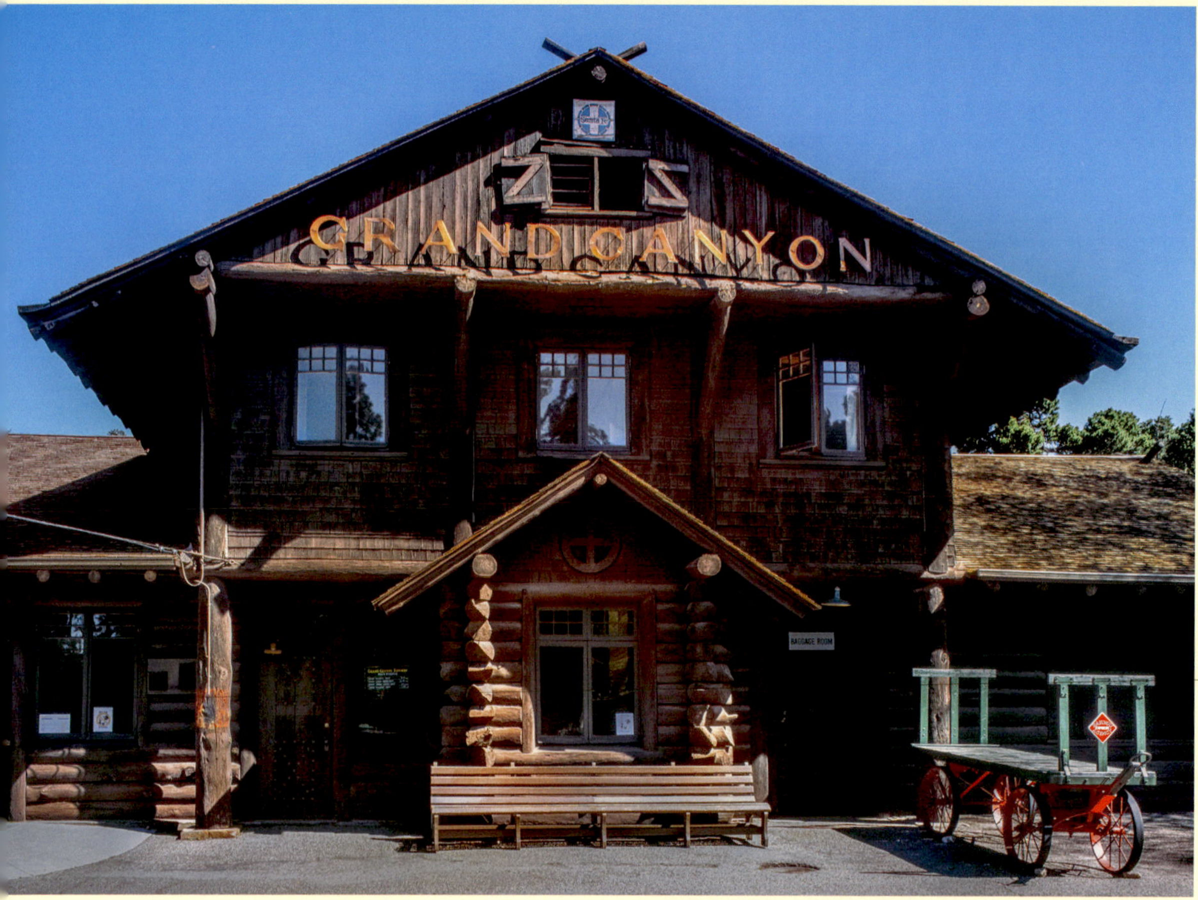

Above: The Grand Canyon Railway, a 64-mile line from Williams, Arizona, disembarks passengers at the timbered train depot in Grand Canyon Village.

Right: Grand Canyon National Park is home to five species of rattlesnake. Highly venomous and best viewed at a distance, most are temperamental only when disturbed.

Far right: Mule riders enjoy a classic western landscape while descending the Bright Angel Trail from the South Rim.

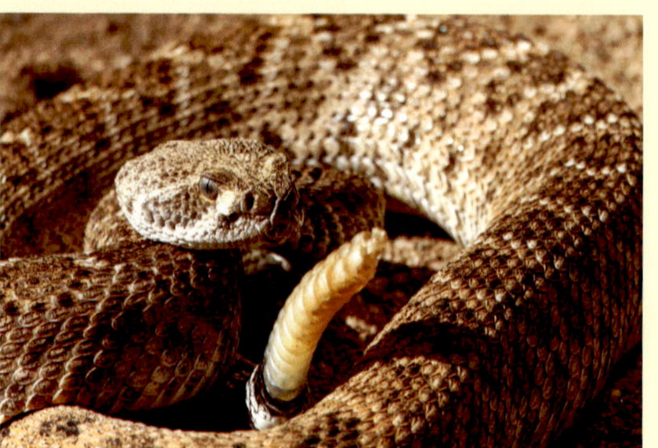

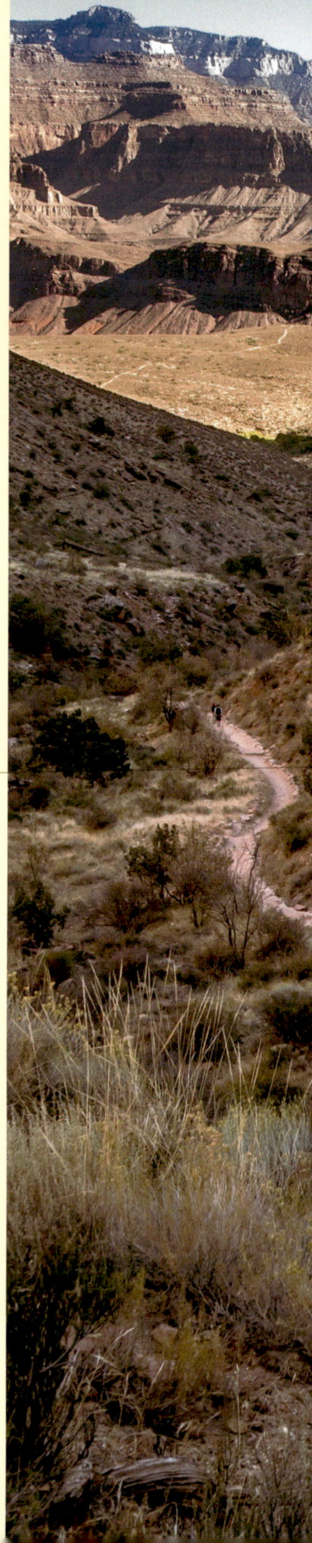

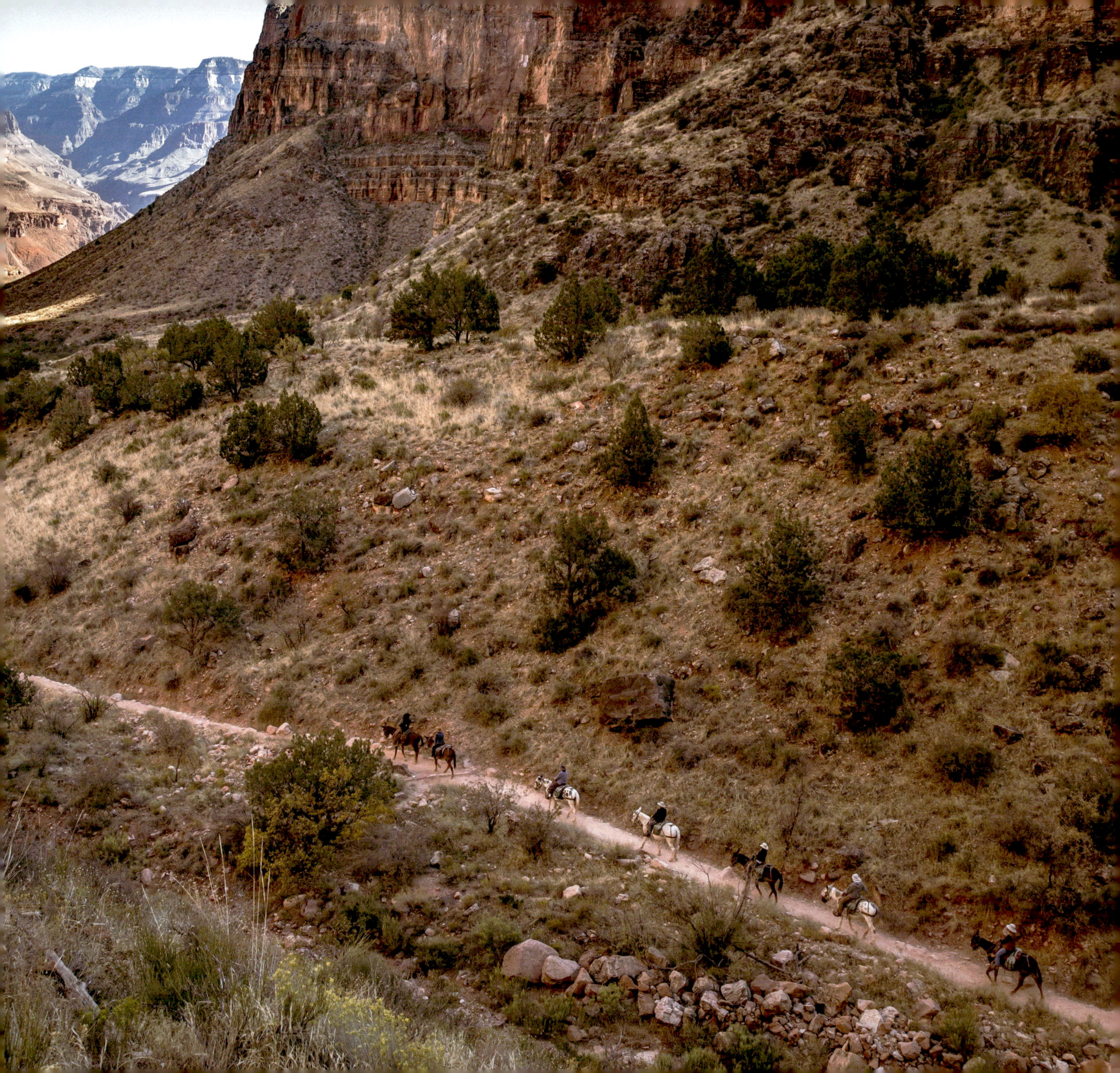

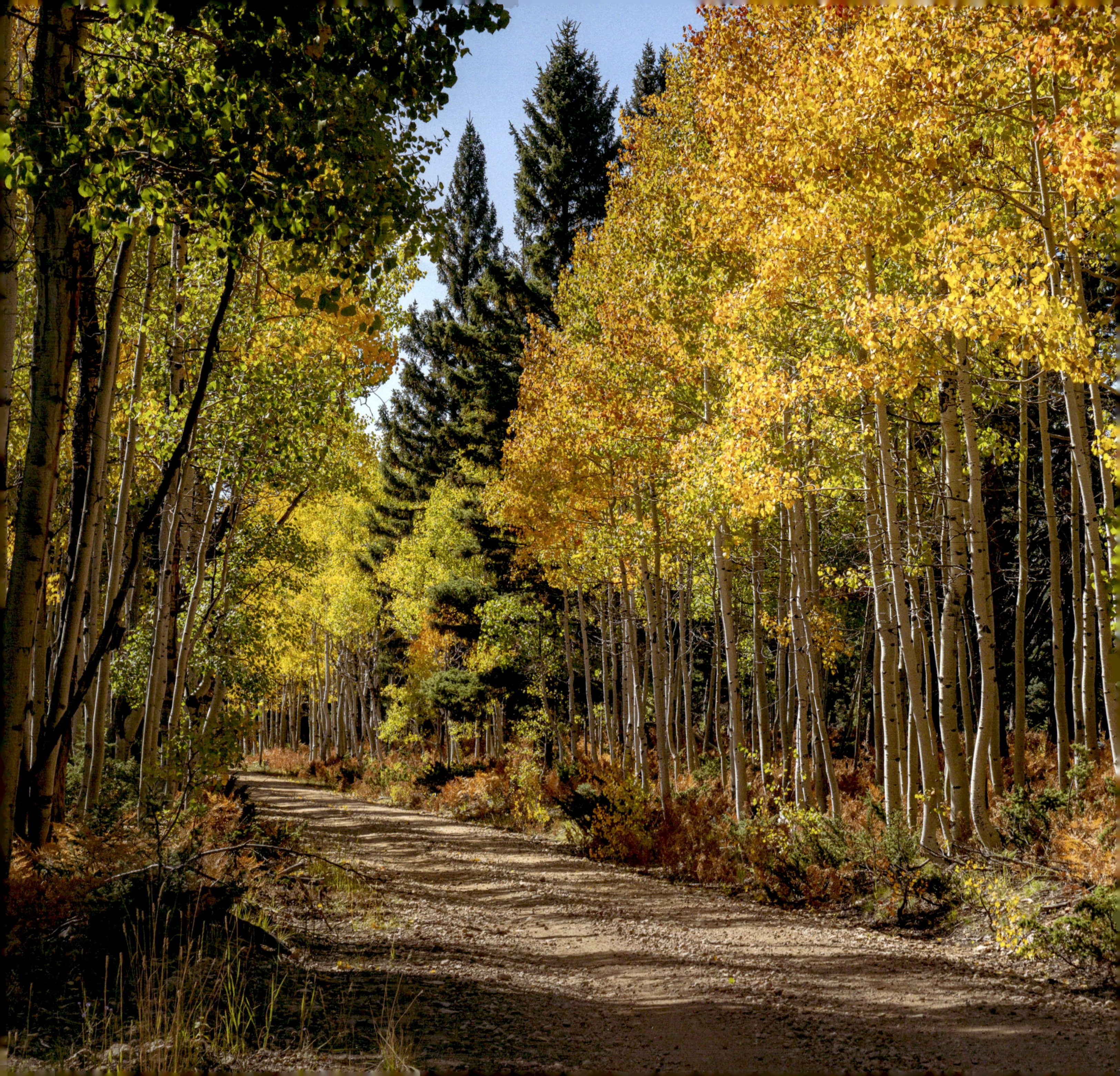

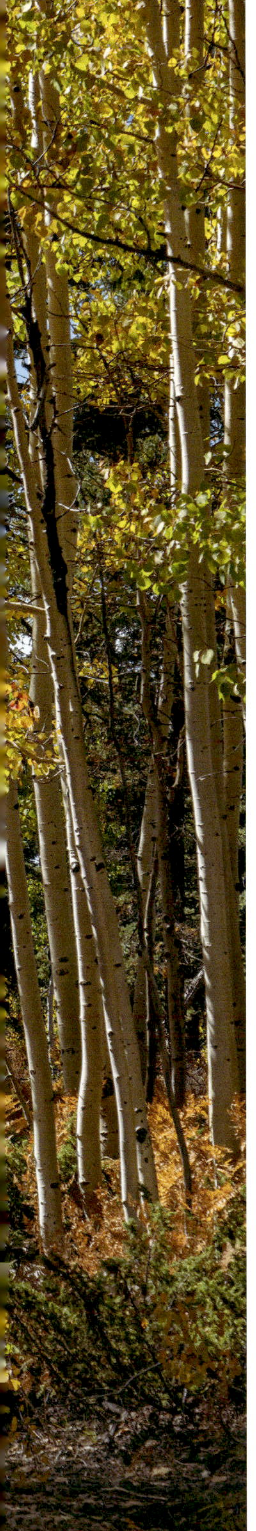

Left: Aspen line a North Rim gravel road in the Kaibab National Forest, which abuts Grand Canyon National Park.

Below: Introduced to the park in 1906, bison readily adapted to life on the Kaibab Plateau. Today, the park service is relocating some bison, reducing the herd size to protect environmental and cultural resources.

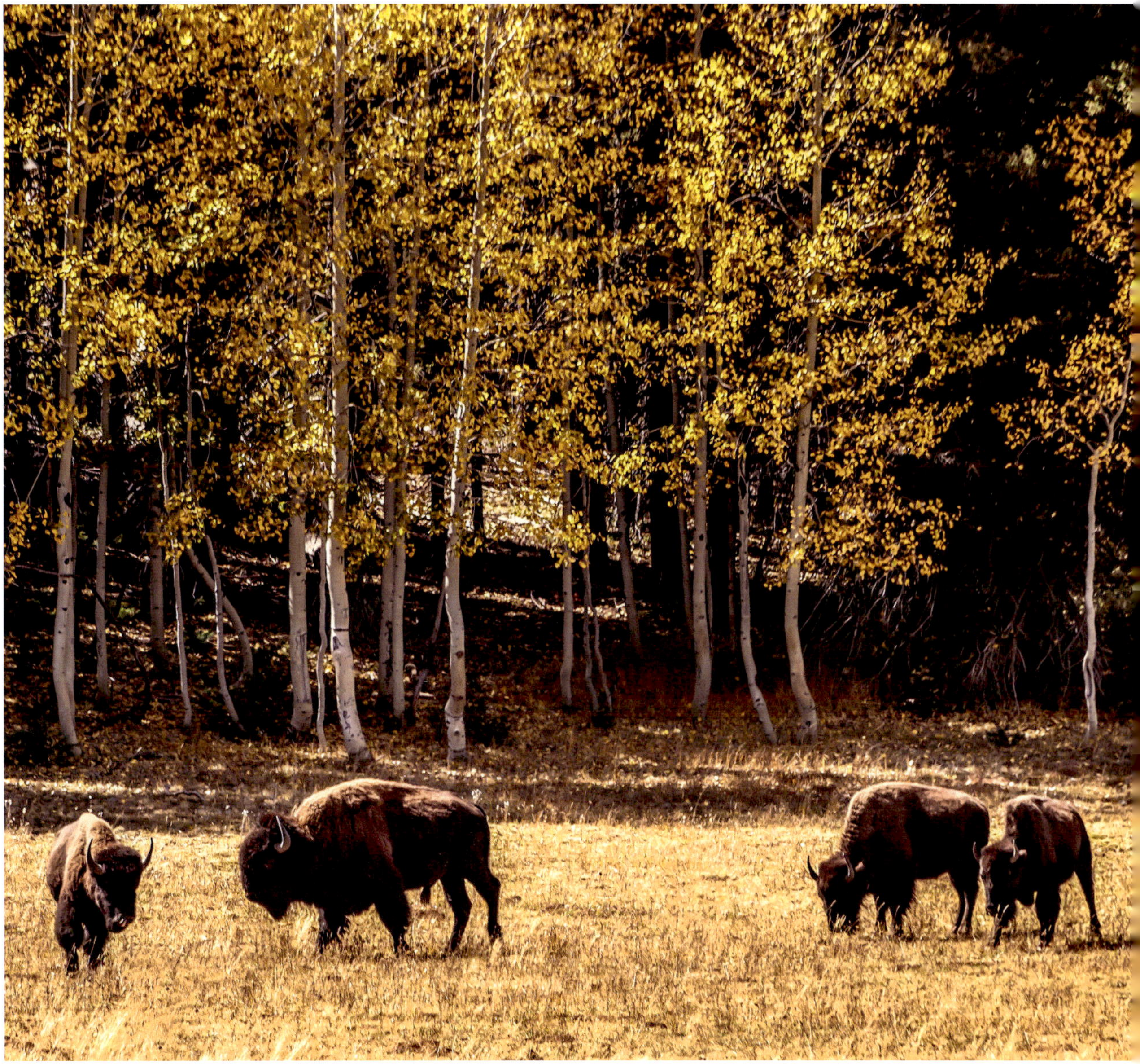

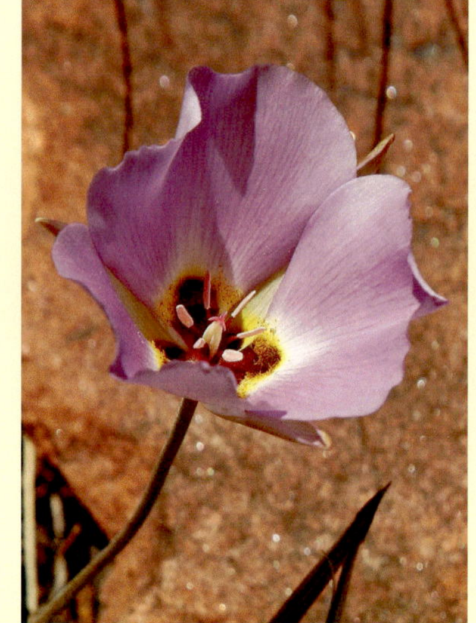

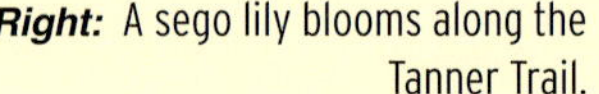

Right: A sego lily blooms along the Tanner Trail.

Far right: The Desert View Watchtower presides over a quiet winter landscape on the South Rim.

Below: The flowers of *Mirabilis jalapa* usually open in the late afternoon, giving rise to its common name, the Four O'Clock flower.

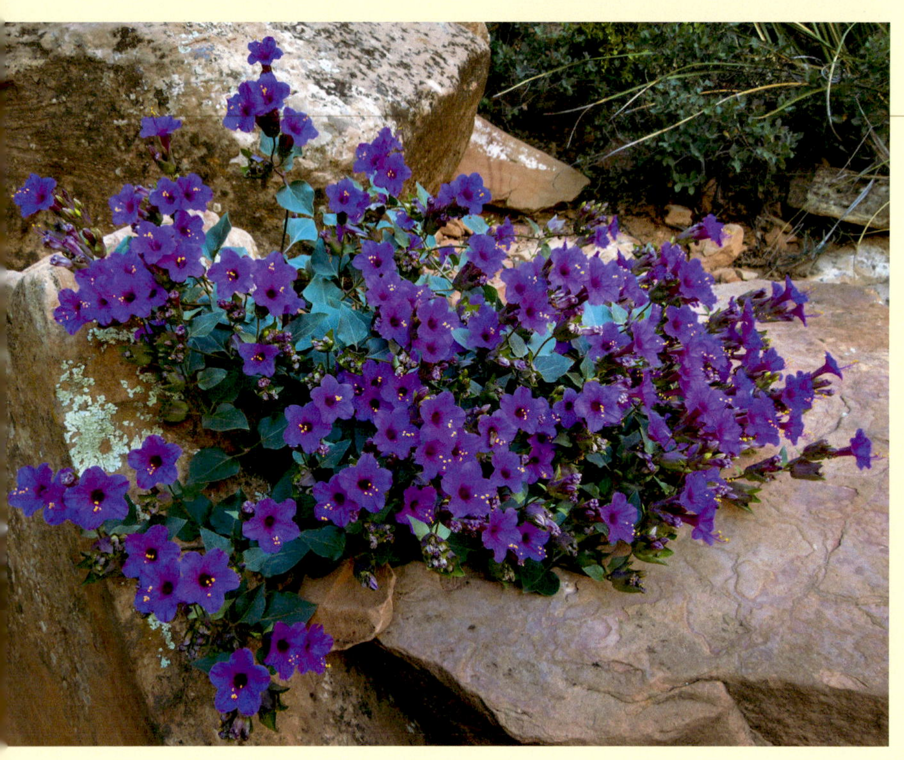

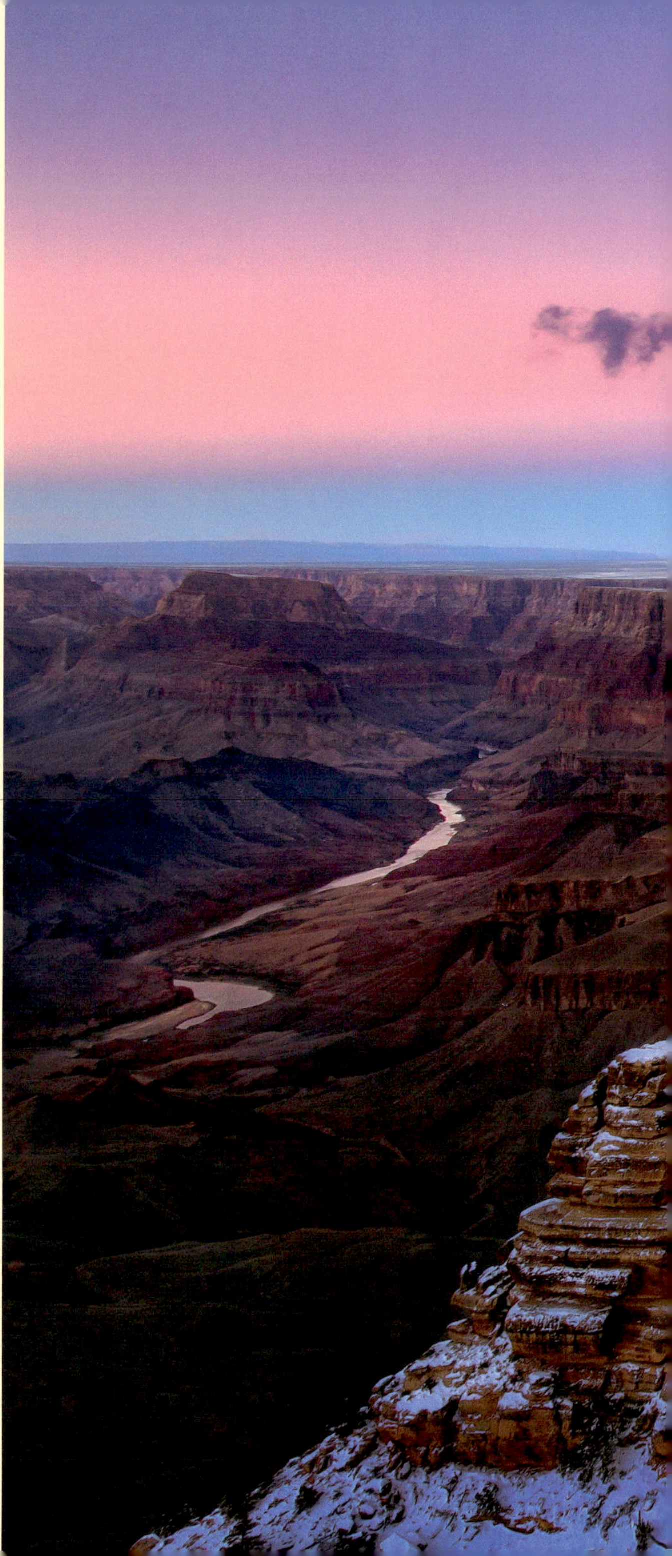

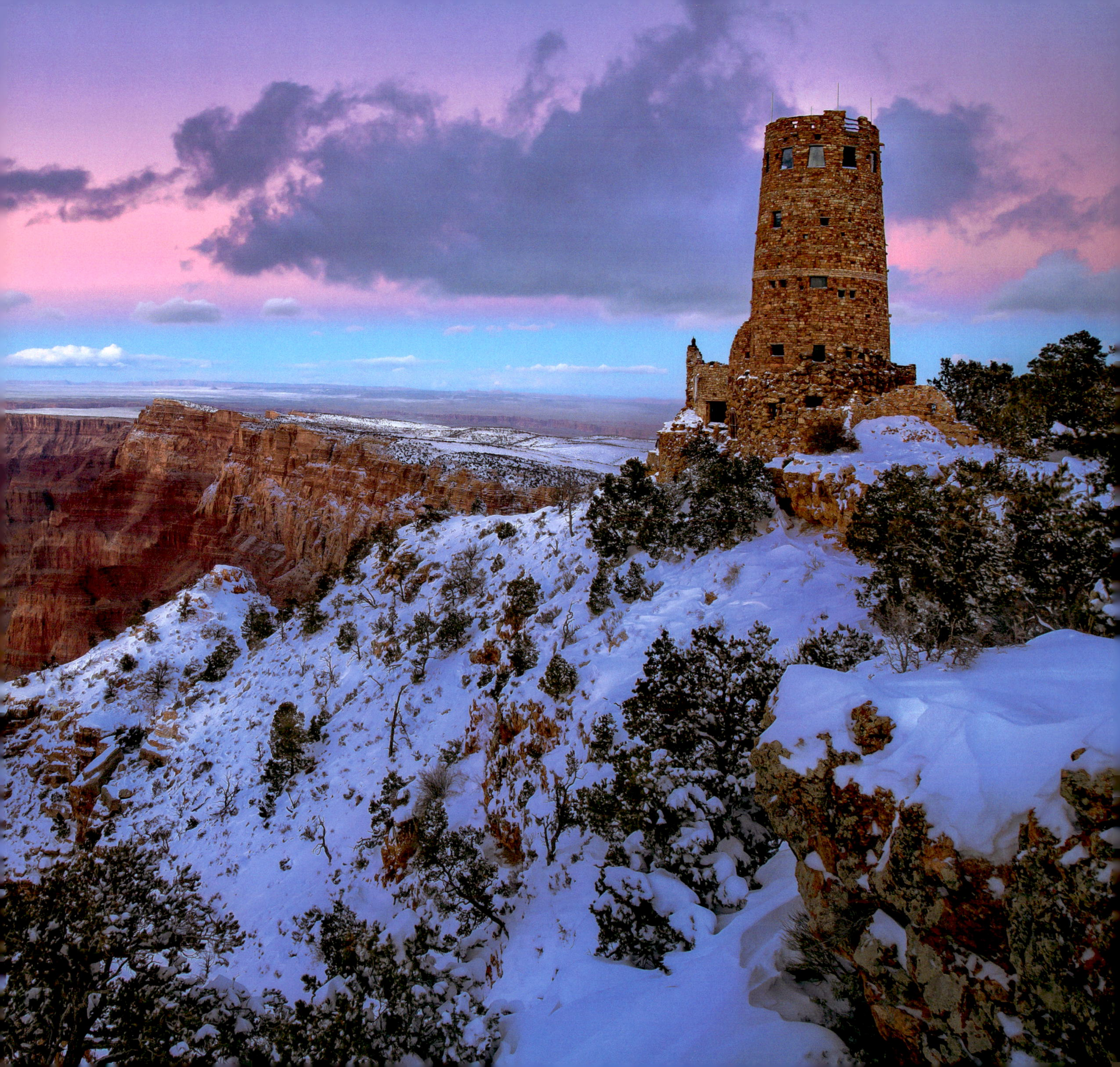

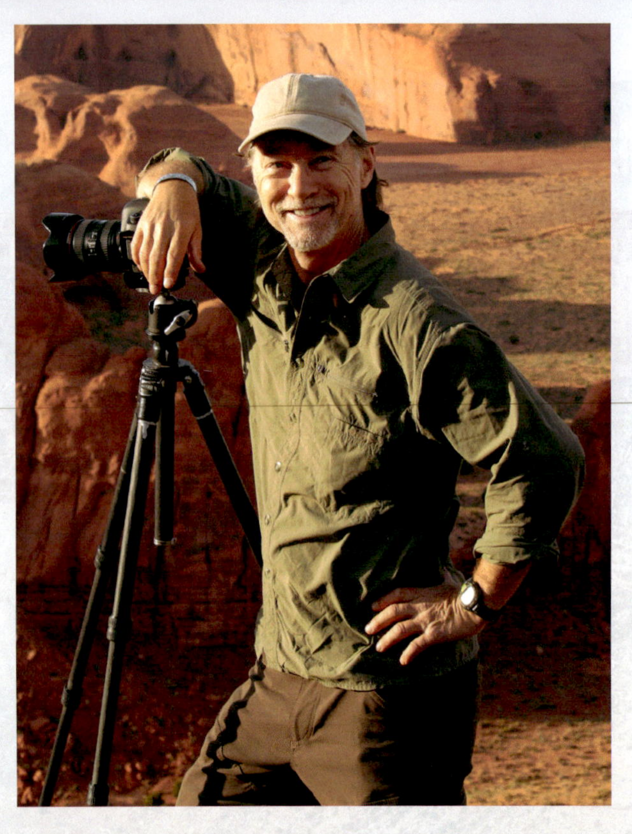

LARRY LINDAHL aims to inspire people with his vibrant, engaging, and thoughtful photography. With over thirty years of experience, he has collected a diverse portfolio from his Grand Canyon backpacking excursions, day hikes, and river trips.

One of his favorite adventures was hiking from the South Rim to the Colorado River without a trail. His party started from the remote Point Huetzl on a five-day outing to access Elves Chasm in unhurried solitude to photograph the enchanted waterfall.

In the course of his other adventures, Larry has rowed an 18-foot oar boat the 225-mile length of Grand Canyon. He has summited Cheops Temple, canyoneered the length of Phantom Creek, explored the Thunder River cave, and slept on Shiva Temple always seeking the perfect photograph.

Outdoor Photographer magazine praised his passion for both photography and the natural world, saying that he "works to tune in to the emotions elicited by a place in order to shape the photographs he makes of it."

His images have been featured in several books about the Grand Canyon including *Lasting Light: 125 Years of Grand Canyon Photography, Grand Canyon: The Vault of Heaven*, and *Grand Reflections*.

His photography reflects his individual relationship with the landscape and is published in magazines such as *Backpacker, American Archaeology, Condé Nast Traveler, Los Angeles Magazine, Der Spiegel, Southwest Art,* and *Arizona Highways*.

He has completed several award-winning books that honor the ancient Native American sites of the Southwest, Sedona, Route 66, and national parks and national monuments of the Four Corners region.

Larry currently resides in Sedona, Arizona, which has been his home for over thirty years. To learn more about his photography, visit LarryLindahl.com.

Background photo: East Rim trail.